# Design:Logo

An exploration of
marvelous marks,
insightful essays and
revealing reviews

**Rockport Publishers**
100 Cummings Center, Suite 406L
Beverly, MA 01915

rockpub.com • rockpaperink.com

Paul Howalt
**Von Glitschka**

# Contents

# Introduction

We can all respect the heritage of the ubiquitous logos of corporate giants such as Samsung, McDonald's, Walmart, Facebook, IBM, and Sony; but as designers, we realize that so many of these marks for large entities show obvious signs of being pushed, pulled, strangled, and beaten into creative submission and sterility. No matter how much the initial brief may tout the brand as being personable and able to provide an emotional connection to a community, the logo ends up reflecting none of the human qualities it brags about. The resulting logo ends up being merely an expensive, impotent placeholder—unoffensive yet uninspiring. This book is not about any of these.

On the other hand, there are logos that grab us by the eyeballs, hug our souls, endear our senses, and don't let go. If you're one who has chosen graphic design and branding for a living, we doubt that you've been inspired to do so by the creative battles that produced marks for any of the corporations named above. I'd venture a guess that most of us were motivated by logos that displayed distinctively clever visual concepts, told a story, or were rendered with industry-defining style. I'm talking about logos such as the old Milwaukee Brewers "ball and glove" monogram from the '70s, the Armor All Viking brand character, the Baskin Robbins "31 flavors" mark, the Android OS logo, the Twitter bird and the Atlanta Falcons "F" symbol. We all recognize these logos as being brilliant, conceptual, and bold. We marvel at these marks, smile, and can't look away. We embrace them with open arms. We run to become members of their brand tribes. They are, in a word, *irresistible*.

Competitive brands are finding the need to court their customer and communicate their message quicker and more thoroughly. That's a tricky tightrope to walk. Every detail and attribute of a logo needs to be carefully scrutinized before incorporating into the final mark. A logo is no longer a simple guarantee of quality and consistency. These days an organization's logo needs to promise a specific emotional experience as well as a connection to a particular community. Logos must be much more than they have been in the past, especially when removed from the context of their supporting visual language. Winning loyalty is secondary; getting them to fall in love is primary.

There will always be a polarized school of thought when it comes to discussing the correct approach to logo design and development. In the end, we know that a successful logo design is not about what pleases the client—its about a mark that works. It's about solving a visual problem. Actually, it's about solving a bunch of problems.

• Does the logo resonate in the souls of your target audience?
• Is it memorably simple, but not boring?
• Is the style appropriate within its industry?
• Is it more timeless than trendy?
• Can you tell a story about it?
• Is it visually clever or conceptual in some way?
• Can it (or a version of it) be reproduced easily across all media?
• Do you want to lick it?

I think we are starting to witness more designers stepping up their games with logo solutions that trade in geometric, corporatized abstraction for custom-tailored creations. Let's celebrate what they do, figure out how they do it, and be inspired to create more ourselves.

— **Paul Howalt and Von Glitschka**

1

# NAUTILUS

®

2

4

**BY RE**

3

5

6

7

**1:** COMPANY: Art Chantry Design / CLIENT: Dave Crider, Estrus Records / DESIGNER: Art Chantry
**2:** COMPANY: Chris Trivizas / CLIENT: Christos & Tassos Manesis / DESIGNER: Chris Trivizas / ART DIRECTOR: Chris Trivizas
**3:** COMPANY: Fernandez Studio / CLIENT: Lost Cowboys / DESIGNER: Carlos Fernandez / ART DIRECTOR: Anita Cleland, Wes Spiker
**4:** COMPANY: Fernandez Studio / DESIGNER: Carlos Fernandez / ART DIRECTORS: Rich Gaidel, Alan Deeter
**5:** COMPANY: Melodic Firtue / CLIENT: Byre / DESIGNER: Aaron Tanner / ART DIRECTOR: Aaron Tanner
**6:** COMPANY: Pollard Design / DESIGNER: Jeff Pollard
**7:** COMPANY: REACTOR design Studio / CLIENT: Julie Wei, MD / DESIGNERS: Julie Sebby, Chase Wilson / ART DIRECTOR: Clifton Alexander

ado
blowout lounge

WINSTED ARTS COUNCIL

CHITTY CHITTY BANG BANG

8

9

10

LIFE IS CHURCH IS LIFE

11

FRESHWATER
Kids

Hamburger
Helper

12

13

8: COMPANY: REACTOR design Studio / CLIENT: Ado Blow Dry Lounge / DESIGNERS: Julie Sebby, Chase Wilson / ART DIRECTOR: Clifton Alexander
9: COMPANY: Schwartzrock Graphic Arts / CLIENT: Winsted Arts Council / DESIGNER: Sherwin Schwartzrock
10: COMPANY: Device / CLIENT: Macmillan Publishing / DESIGNER: Rian Hughes / ART DIRECTOR: Rachel Vale
11: COMPANY: Fernandez Studio / CLIENT: Lincoln Park Zoo / DESIGNER: Carlos Fernandez / ART DIRECTOR: Peggy Martin
12: COMPANY: Schwartzrock Graphic Arts / CLIENT: Freshwater Church / DESIGNER: Sherwin Schwartzrock
13: COMPANY: Glischka Studios / CLIENT: Brandimage / DESIGNER: Von Glitschka / ART DIRECTOR: Tamara Kramer

14

15

16

17

18

19

20

21

**14:** COMPANY: Gardner Design / CLIENT: Danse Arte / DESIGNER: Brian Miller / ART DIRECTOR: Brian Miller
**15:** COMPANY: REACTOR design Studio / CLIENT: REACTOR design studio / DESIGNER: Chase Wilson / ART DIRECTOR: Clifton Alexander
**16:** COMPANY: Dotzero Design / CLIENT: Lucia / DESIGNERS: Jon Wippich, Karen Wippich / ART DIRECTORS: Jon Wippich, Karen Wippich
**17:** COMPANY: Melodic Firtue / CLIENT: Open Shut / DESIGNER: Aaron Tanner / ART DIRECTOR: Aaron Tanner
**18:** COMPANY: Dotzero Design / CLIENT: Live Wire Radio / DESIGNERS: Jon Wippich, Karen Wippich / ART DIRECTORS: Jon Wippich, Karen Wippich
**19:** COMPANY: Melodic Firtue / CLIENT: Burnt Prairie Print Shop / DESIGNER: Aaron Tanner / ART DIRECTOR: Aaron Tanner
**20:** COMPANY: Design Center, Inc. / CLIENT: DSI / DESIGNER: Sherwin Schwartzrock / ART DIRECTOR: John Reger
**21:** COMPANY: Duct Tape & Glitter / CLIENT: Abby's Gift / DESIGNER: Luke Bott

22

23

24

25

26

27

28

29

**MULTICOURSE**™

31

*Sunrise*

**KITCHEN**

30

MOUNTAIN
**MOUTH**
*Dollywood*
THE KINDA FUN THAT'LL CHANGE YER SPEAKIN!

32

CANDLE BOOKS

33

**MANAO** LABS

34

35

36

**30:** COMPANY: R&R Partners / CLIENT: Tony Thielen / DESIGNER: Randy Heil / ART DIRECTOR: Randy Heil
**31:** COMPANY: Bravo Company / CLIENT: Multicourse / DESIGNER: Amanda Ho / ART DIRECTOR: Edwin Tan
**32:** COMPANY: U! Creative Inc. / CLIENT: Dollywood - Mountain Mouth / DESIGNER: U! Creative Team
**33:** COMPANY: Luke Bott Design & Illustration / DESIGNER: Luke Bott
**34:** COMPANY: Yona Lee Design Studio / CLIENT: Manao Labs / DESIGNERS: Yona Lee, Alvaro Del Canto / ART DIRECTOR: Yona Lee
**35:** COMPANY: Gardner Design / CLIENT: Stack-On / DESIGNER: Adam Anderson / ART DIRECTOR: Brian Miller
**36:** COMPANY: Yona Lee Design Studio / CLIENT: Yona Lee / DESIGNERS: Alvaro Del Canto, Matthieu Visentin / ART DIRECTOR: Yona Lee

# zynga

37

38

**Bee Alive**

39

41

40

TommyKnocker

42

HISTORY THEATRE

**37:** COMPANY: Odopod / CLIENT: Zynga / DESIGNER: Felix Sockwell / ART DIRECTOR: Guthrie Dolan
**38:** COMPANY: Fernandez Studio / CLIENT: Penco Construction / DESIGNER: Carlos Fernandez / ART DIRECTOR: Carlos Fernandez
**39:** COMPANY: Schwartzrock Graphic Arts / CLIENT: Acsent Marketing / DESIGNER: Sherwin Schwartzrock
**40:** COMPANY: Glischka Studios / CLIENT: Barnhart / DESIGNER: Von Glitschka / ART DIRECTOR: Jim Hargreaves
**41:** COMPANY: Esser Design / CLIENT: Self Care / DESIGNER: Paul Howalt / ART DIRECTOR: Danny Neuman
**42:** COMPANY: Schwartzrock Graphic Arts / CLIENT: Design Center / DESIGNER: Sherwin Schwartzrock

43

44

45

46

47

48

49

50

43: COMPANY: Art Chantry Design / CLIENT: Dave Crider, Estrus Records / DESIGNER: Art Chantry / ART DIRECTOR: Art Chantry
44: COMPANY: Schwartzrock Graphic Arts / CLIENT: Freshwater Church / DESIGNER: Sherwin Schwartzrock
45: COMPANY: Schwartzrock Graphic Arts / CLIENT: Community Comics / DESIGNER: Sherwin Schwartzrock
46: COMPANY: DesignUnion / CLIENT: MobCraft Beer / DESIGNER: Renee Melton
47: COMPANY: chameleon design / CLIENT: Slavo Antos / DESIGNER: Tomas Vateha / ART DIRECTOR: Tomas Vateha
48: COMPANY: Fernandez Studio / CLIENT: Prefco Distribution / DESIGNER: Carlos Fernandez / ART DIRECTOR: Kristin Moses
49: COMPANY: Tactix Creative, Inc. / CLIENT: Nestea / DESIGNER: Paul Howalt
50: COMPANY: Fernandez Studio / CLIENT: MojoLingo / DESIGNER: Carlos Fernandez / ART DIRECTORS: Rich Goidel, Alan Deeter

51

**SHIELDWOLF**

52

53

54

INVEST
COLLEGIATE

55

56

57

58

**51:** COMPANY: Gardner Design / CLIENT: Virtual Focus / DESIGNER: Chris Parks / ART DIRECTOR: Brian Miller
**52:** COMPANY: Glischka Studios / CLIENT: Randy Caldejon / DESIGNER: Von Glitschka / ART DIRECTOR: Von Glitschka
**53:** COMPANY: Fernandez Studio / DESIGNER: Carlos Fernandez / ART DIRECTORS: Rich Goidel, Alan Deeter
**54:** COMPANY: Fernandez Studio / CLIENT: Killian's / DESIGNER: Carlos Fernandez / ART DIRECTOR: Mike Johnson
**55:** COMPANY: Little / CLIENT: Invest Collegiate / DESIGNER: Jason Richardson / ART DIRECTOR: Santiago Crespo
**56:** COMPANY: Gardner Design / CLIENT: Youthville / DESIGNER: Brian Weins / ART DIRECTOR: Brian Miller
**57:** COMPANY: Fernandez Studio / CLIENT: Courtney Construction / DESIGNER: Carlos Fernandez / ART DIRECTOR: Steve Rodin
**58:** COMPANY: chameleon design / CLIENT: Ondrei Teraz / DESIGNER: Tomas Vateha / ART DIRECTOR: Tomas Vateha

# A Closer Look

**FIRM:** CHRIS PARKS
**DESIGNER / ILLUSTRATOR:** CHRIS PARKS
**ART DIRECTOR:** CHRIS PARKS
**CLIENT:** THE ANCHOR

A favorite client of mine asked me to develop a promotional logo which celebrated the anniversary of her gastro pub, the Anchor. The client is an abstract thinker and lover of local civic history. She loved the idea of celebrating a novelty product called The Hop Rod, that was made in Wichita, Kansas, in the early '70s by Chance Manufacturing. This little gizmo was a crazy gas-powered pogo stick that never really took off. My task was to try to bring the two notions together and somehow not confuse the hell out of her patrons.

In a fit of desperation, interspersed with a moment of fear, I meditated on the inherent visual qualities of the hop rod and EUREKA! I conceptualized a vertical shaft, with horizontal extrusions on both the top and bottom, similar to an anchor.

To make the solution more playful, a rider was considered. This became an obvious way for further connection with the nautical theme of the pub. The final visual became a metaphor on how my client viewed her business—a unique machine that grew and gained momentum, as she added fuel.

*The Anchor logo and the Hop Rod form seem destined to be combined into one stunning mark. Parks picks up on this and deepens the visual concept at every turn. He graphically represents the beer hops visual pun on the anchor shaft and translates the toy's foot pegs and handlebars into anchor prongs.*

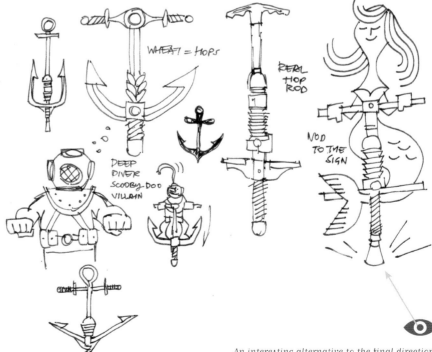

*An interesting alternative to the final direction. Parks pairs the original mermaid from the anchor logo with the Hop Rod, but renders her form in a very snappy '70s line-art style. With his illustrative skills, I think Parks could have made this direction just as successful.*

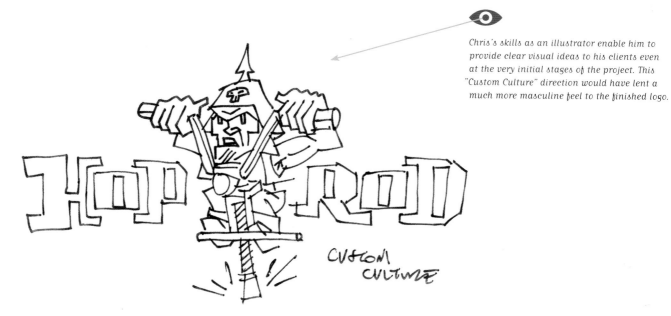

 Chris's skills as an illustrator enable him to provide clear visual ideas to his clients even at the very initial stages of the project. This "Custom Culture" direction would have lent a much more masculine feel to the finished logo.

CUSTOM CULTURE

Parks builds all his logos with a brilliant optical balance between positive and negative space. This mark borders on being a spot illustration, but because of the simplified graphic rendering style and reducibility, it succeeds in either camp. As you can see, this logo has the perfect amount of detail to make a very engaging T-shirt even without any additional embellishment.

59

60

61

**BRASSERIE**

62

63

64

Westwood

65

**59:** COMPANY: Art Chantry Design / CLIENT: Dave Crider, Estrus Records / DESIGNER: Art Chantry / ART DIRECTOR: Art Chantry
**60:** COMPANY: Luke Bott Design & Illustration / CLIENT: Ashley Brooks Piercing / DESIGNER: Luke Bott
**61:** COMPANY: Pacey + Pacey Design / CLIENT: Manta World Sport / DESIGNER: Michael Pacey / ART DIRECTOR: Robert Pacey
**62:** COMPANY: Bravo Company / CLIENT: Balzac Brasserie / DESIGNER: Amando Ho / ART DIRECTOR: Edwin Tan
**63:** COMPANY: Glischka Studios / CLIENT: Street 2 Street / DESIGNER: Von Glitschka / ART DIRECTOR: Von Glitschka
**64:** COMPANY: Jon Flaming Design / CLIENT: David Arrington / DESIGNER: Jon Flaming / ART DIRECTOR: Jon Flaming
**65:** COMPANY: Schwartzrock Graphic Arts / CLIENT: Westwood Lutheran Church / DESIGNER: Sherwin Schwartzrock / ART DIRECTOR: Sherwin Schwartzrock

66

67

68

69

70

71

72

66: COMPANY: Subzero Design / CLIENT: The Sacred Spur / DESIGNER: Paul Howalt / ART DIRECTOR: Bill Leissring
67: COMPANY: U! Creative Inc. / CLIENT: Monsterus - Rock Band Identity / DESIGNER: U! Creative Team
68: COMPANY: Pollard Design / CLIENT: Nike Womens X Training / DESIGNER: Jeff Pollard
69: COMPANY: Fernandez Studio / CLIENT: Laughing Angels Foundation / DESIGNER: Carlos Fernandez / ART DIRECTOR: Mike Wilson
70: COMPANY: Banowetz & Company / CLIENT: El Fenix Tex-Mex Express / DESIGNER: Sarah Terrell / ART DIRECTOR: Eric Venegas
71: COMPANY: Device / CLIENT: DC Comics / DESIGNER: Rian Hughes / ART DIRECTOR: Kenny Lopez
72: COMPANY: Device / CLIENT: Fiell Publishing / DESIGNER: Rian Hughes / ART DIRECTOR: Rian Hughes

## Dr. Stacie Ross

[rhymes with *floss*]

**73**

## AVONLEA

FLORAL ARTS

**74**

**75**

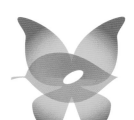

**76**

## Schottenstein

PROPERTY GROUP

**77**

**78**

**79**

**80**

**73:** COMPANY: Pacey + Pacey Design / CLIENT: Dr. Stacie Ross, DMD / DESIGNER: Michael Pacey / ART DIRECTOR: Robert Pacey
**74:** COMPANY: Design Center, Inc. / CLIENT: Avonlea Floral Arts / DESIGNER: Sherwin Schwartzrock / ART DIRECTOR: John Reger
**75:** COMPANY: Tim Frame Design / CLIENT: Brentwood Builders / DESIGNER: Tim Frame / ART DIRECTOR: Tim Frame
**76:** COMPANY: Schwartzrock Graphic Arts / CLIENT: BI Worldwide / DESIGNER: Sherwin Schwartzrock / ART DIRECTOR: Sherwin Schwartzrock
**77:** COMPANY: Tim Frame Design / CLIENT: Schottenstein Property Group / DESIGNER: Tim Frame / ART DIRECTOR: Rebecca Reeder
**78:** COMPANY: Schwartzrock Graphic Arts / CLIENT: BI Worldwide / DESIGNER: Sherwin Schwartzrock
**79:** COMPANY: Schwartzrock Graphic Arts / CLIENT: Kingstone Media / DESIGNER: Sherwin Schwartzrock
**80:** COMPANY: Invisible Creature / CLIENT: Invisible Creature / DESIGNER: Ryan Clark / ART DIRECTOR: Ryan Clark

81

82

83

84

85

86

87

88

81: COMPANY: Schwartzrock Graphic Arts / CLIENT: Target / DESIGNER: Sherwin Schwartzrock
82: COMPANY: Schwartzrock Graphic Arts / CLIENT: Design Center / DESIGNER: Sherwin Schwartzrock
83: COMPANY: Design Center, Inc. / CLIENT: Byerly's and Lunds / DESIGNER: Sherwin Schwartzrock / ART DIRECTOR: John Reger
84: COMPANY: Device / CLIENT: Marvel / DESIGNER: Rian Hughes / ART DIRECTORS: Axel Alonzo, John Barber
85: COMPANY: U! Creative Inc. / CLIENT: Rockives / DESIGNER: U! Creative Team / ART DIRECTOR:
86: COMPANY: Schwartzrock Graphic Arts / CLIENT: BI Worldwide / DESIGNER: Sherwin Schwartzrock
87: COMPANY: Schwartzrock Graphic Arts / CLIENT: AIGA Minnesota / DESIGNER: Sherwin Schwartzrock
88: COMPANY: Invisible Creature / CLIENT: The Presidents Of The United States Of America / DESIGNER: Ryan Clark / ART DIRECTOR: Ryan Clark

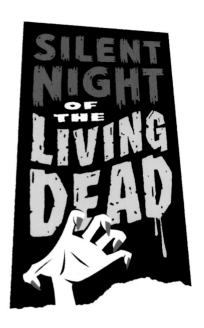

89

90

91

METRO
PRAYZ

92

93

94

95

**89:** COMPANY: Device / CLIENT: Gingerbread Monkey / DESIGNER: Rian Hughes / ART DIRECTOR: Colin Smith
**90:** COMPANY: Schwartzrock Graphic Arts / CLIENT: Blackwood Management Group / DESIGNER: Sherwin Schwartzrock
**91:** COMPANY: Schwartzrock Graphic Arts / CLIENT: Kingstone Media / DESIGNER: Sherwin Schwartzrock
**92:** CLIENT: Keith Everson / DESIGNER: Mike Jones
**93:** COMPANY: Tactix Creative, Inc. / CLIENT: Metro Prayz Logo / DESIGNER: Paul Howalt
**94:** COMPANY: U! Creative, Inc. / CLIENT: Pies & Pints Pizzeria / DESIGNER: U! Creative Team
**95:** COMPANY: Invisible Creature / CLIENT: All American Rejects / DESIGNER: Ryan Clark / ART DIRECTOR: Ryan Clark

96

97

98

99

100

101

96: COMPANY: Owen Jones Design / CLIENT: Katalistik / DESIGNER: Owen Jones / ART DIRECTOR: Owen Jones
97: COMPANY: Schwartzrock Graphic Arts / CLIENT: Chalk, Inc. / DESIGNER: Sherwin Schwartzrock
98: COMPANY: U! Creative, Inc. / CLIENT: Boonshoft Museum of Discovery / DESIGNER: U! Creative Team
99: COMPANY: Tactix Creative, Inc. / CLIENT: Lucky 57 Customs / DESIGNER: Paul Howalt
100: COMPANY: Schwartzrock Graphic Arts / CLIENT: Freshwater Church / DESIGNER: Sherwin Schwartzrock
101: COMPANY: Tactix Creative, Inc. / CLIENT: City of Phoenix / DESIGNER: Paul Howalt

102

103

104

105

106

107

108

109

102: COMPANY: D. Studio 21 / CLIENT: Chartwells / DESIGNER: Paul Howalt / ART DIRECTOR: Heather Jordan
103: COMPANY: Star Group / CLIENT: AMNRL / DESIGNER: Scott Oeschger / ART DIRECTOR: Scott Oeschger
104: COMPANY: Tactix Creative, Inc. / CLIENT: Vision West Community / DESIGNER: Paul Howalt
105: COMPANY: Schwartzrock Graphic Arts / CLIENT: Jim Nash / DESIGNER: Sherwin Schwartzrock
106: COMPANY: Salvadore Anguiano / CLIENT: Dá Fro Clothing / DESIGNER: Salvadore Anguiano / ART DIRECTOR: Salvadore Anguiano
107: COMPANY: Funnel Design Group / CLIENT: Sound Cubed / DESIGNER: Taylor Goad
108: COMPANY: Work Labs / CLIENT: Elephant Pharm / DESIGNER: Paul Howalt / ART DIRECTOR: Cabell Harris
109: COMPANY: Fernandez Studio / CLIENT: SIMA Financial Group / DESIGNER: Carlos Fernandez / ART DIRECTOR: Mark Smith

110

111

112

113

114

115

116

117

110: COMPANY: Grupo Habermas Comunicación / CLIENT: San Antonio / DESIGNER: Jerónimo Atienza / ART DIRECTOR: Fernando Suárez
111: COMPANY: Wonderwheel Creative / CLIENT: Zofia & Co. / DESIGNER: Sarah Lotus Trainor / ART DIRECTOR: Tim Merrill
112: COMPANY: Jared Granger / CLIENT: Exploration / DESIGNER: Jared Granger / ART DIRECTOR: Jared Granger
113: COMPANY: Tactix Creative, Inc. / CLIENT: Smith Real Estate / DESIGNER: Paul Howalt
114: COMPANY: Device / CLIENT: Marvel / DESIGNER: Rian Hughes / ART DIRECTOR: Lauren Sankovitch
115: COMPANY: Schwartzrock Graphic Arts / CLIENT: BI Worldwide / DESIGNER: Sherwin Schwartzrock
116: COMPANY: Schwartzrock Graphic Arts / CLIENT: Initio3i / DESIGNER: Sherwin Schwartzrock
117: COMPANY: Scott Oeschger / CLIENT: Cole Matthew Oeschger / DESIGNER: Scott Oeschger / ART DIRECTOR: Scott Oeschger

**FIRM:** FERNANDEZ STUDIO
**DESIGNER / ILLUSTRATOR:** CARLOS FERNANDEZ
**ART DIRECTOR:** STEVE LALIBERTE
**CLIENT:** MISSOURI DEPARTMENT OF TOURISM

I was contacted by an ad agency tasked with rebranding the state of Missouri. The concept, derived from Missouri's nickname as "The Show-Me State," featured an arc filled with a collage of Missouri attractions. This arc of Missouri goodies would have to include the cities of St. Louis, Kansas City, and Branson, in addition to the state's natural features such as parks, lakes, caves, hills, etc.

My first step was to research and gather image references for all of the logo's elements. During this process, I learned Missouri's state bird and flower, and immediately knew I wanted to incorporate them into the illustration to add warmth and personality. Next, I started with some very loose pencil sketches exploring the placement and composition of all the arc's elements. After sharing these roughs with the art director, I was given feedback and direction to proceed.

Next, a tight pencil rendering of the line work details was developed, scanned, and used as a visual guide for the computer illustration process. Once the illustration was complete, type and color exploration were applied until arriving at a favorite combination to send along to the art director for client presentation.

*Inviting, curious, and diverse—these are the attributes this mark imbues in a fun and memorable way.*

*Using the process of thumbnail sketching, the designer solved the visual challenge of balancing the gamut of state landmarks and locations without giving too much attention to any one.*

It's nice to see craftsmanship in analog form. A progressive refinement of an idea predigital lends to the strength of the final mark and its skillful execution.

The nice splash of color and simple type exploration really button up this design well without adding more complexity to the design.

118

119

121

120

122

123

124

**118:** COMPANY: Gardner Design / CLIENT: Mend Physiotherapy / DESIGNER: Ty Wilkins / ART DIRECTOR: Brian Miller
**119:** COMPANY: Gardner Design / CLIENT: Grace Hill Winery / DESIGNER: Luke Bott / ART DIRECTOR: Brian Miller
**120:** COMPANY: Tactix Creative, Inc. / CLIENT: Fulton Brock / DESIGNER: Paul Howalt
**121:** COMPANY: Glischka Studios / CLIENT: Veer / DESIGNER: Von Glitschka / ART DIRECTOR: Von Glitschka
**122:** COMPANY: Jon Flaming Design / CLIENT: VHA / DESIGNER: Jon Flaming / ART DIRECTOR: Jon Flaming
**123:** CLIENT: Felicha DeSpain / DESIGNER: Chris Parks / ART DIRECTOR: Chris Parks
**124:** COMPANY: WORKtoDATE (www.worktodate.com) / CLIENT: Darrin L. Frison / DESIGNER: Greg Bennett / ART DIRECTOR: Greg Bennett

125

126

127

128

129

130

131

**125:** CLIENT: Alex Harb / DESIGNER: Chris Parks / ART DIRECTOR: Chris Parks
**126:** COMPANY: Art Chantry Design / CLIENT: Post-Industrial Stress + Design / DESIGNER: Art Chantry / ART DIRECTOR: Art Chantry
**127:** COMPANY: Gardner Design / CLIENT: Youthville / DESIGNER: Luke Bott / ART DIRECTOR: Brian Miller
**128:** COMPANY: Gardner Design / CLIENT: The Church of the Latter Day Saints / DESIGNER: Bill Gardner / ART DIRECTOR: Bill Gardner
**129:** COMPANY: Bravo Company / CLIENT: Five & Dime Eatery / DESIGNER: Amanda Ho / ART DIRECTOR: Edwin Tan
**130:** COMPANY: Gardner Design / CLIENT: Oaklawn Elementary Cheetahs / DESIGNER: Brian Miller / ART DIRECTOR: Brian Miller
**131:** CLIENT: Marketing Services / DESIGNER: Chris Parks / ART DIRECTOR: Chris Parks, Todd Ramsey, Kenton Hansen

132

133

134

135

136

137

138

139

**132:** COMPANY: Duct Tape & Glitter / CLIENT: Launch Laser / DESIGNER: Luke Bott
**133:** COMPANY: Tim Frame Design / CLIENT: Brantwood Elementary School / DESIGNER: Tim Frame / ART DIRECTOR: Tim Frame
**134:** COMPANY: Thinkcreative Design / CLIENT: / DESIGNER: Todd Hansson / ART DIRECTOR: Marty Towers
**135:** COMPANY: WORKtoDATE (www.worktodate.com) / CLIENT: theCOUNTERcorps (www.thecountercorps.com) / DESIGNER: Greg Bennett / ART DIRECTOR: Greg Bennett
**136:** COMPANY: Schwartzrock Graphic Arts / CLIENT: Andrea Oien / DESIGNER: Sherwin Schwartzrock
**137:** COMPANY: R&R Partners / CLIENT: Envision EMI / DESIGNER: Randy Heil / ART DIRECTOR: Randy Heil
**138:** COMPANY: OYA Group / CLIENT: XL Construction / DESIGNER: Clint G. Delapaz / ART DIRECTOR: Karen Hebert-Gordon
**139:** COMPANY: Invisible Creature / CLIENT: Tooth & Nail Records / DESIGNER: Don Clark / ART DIRECTOR: Don Clark

140

141

142

143

144

COMMUNITY CHRISTIAN
SCHOOL

145

146

147

**140:** COMPANY: Screamin'Yeti Designs / CLIENT: Screamin'Yeti Designs / DESIGNER: Mike Kirkpatrick / ART DIRECTOR: Mike Kirkpatrick
**141:** COMPANY: Mode Design / CLIENT: Lowbrau / DESIGNER: Hans Bennewitz, Ian Ingalis / ART DIRECTOR: Hans Bennewitz, Ian Ingalis
**142:** COMPANY: Device / CLIENT: Matt Haley / DESIGNER: Rian Hughes / ART DIRECTOR: Matt Haley
**143:** COMPANY: U! Creative, Inc. / CLIENT: Progressive Printers Inc. / DESIGNER: U! Creative Team
**144:** COMPANY: Schwartzrock Graphic Arts / CLIENT: BI Worldwide / DESIGNER: Sherwin Schwartzrock
**145:** COMPANY: Schwartzrock Graphic Arts / CLIENT: Christian Community School / DESIGNER: Sherwin Schwartzrock
**146:** COMPANY: Dreambox Creative / CLIENT: Executopia / DESIGNER: Hans Bennewitz / ART DIRECTOR: Doru Bere
**147:** COMPANY: Schwartzrock Graphic Arts / CLIENT: RiverBrand Design / DESIGNER: Sherwin Schwartzrock

148

149

150

151

152

153

154

**148:** COMPANY: Jon Flaming Design / CLIENT: Cattle Baron's Ball/Dallas / DESIGNER: Jon Flaming / ART DIRECTOR: Jon Flaming
**149:** COMPANY: P3 New Media / CLIENT: / DESIGNER: Paul Howalt / ART DIRECTOR: James Payne
**150:** COMPANY: Schwartzrock Graphic Arts / CLIENT: BI Worldwide / DESIGNER: Sherwin Schwartzrock
**151:** COMPANY: Schwartzrock Graphic Arts / CLIENT: 3.2.1. Inc / DESIGNER: Sherwin Schwartzrock
**152:** COMPANY: Design Center, Inc. / CLIENT: Design Center / DESIGNER: Sherwin Schwartzrock / ART DIRECTOR: John Reger
**153:** COMPANY: / CLIENT: Britain Way Apartments / DESIGNER: Paul Howalt
**154:** COMPANY: Mode Design / CLIENT: June Lion / DESIGNER: Hans Bennewitz / ART DIRECTOR: Hans Bennewitz

npn NEW PERFORMANCE NUTRITION

155

ESTB 1982

**BRAUN & BUTLER**

CONSTRUCTION

156

ACA INTERNATIONAL
*Foundation Golf Tournament*
JULY **FGT** 2002
ORLANDO FLORIDA

157

158

159

*Avon Lea*
FLORAL ARTS

160

**RIGGS**
DISTRIBUTING, INC.

**155:** COMPANY: Hatch Design / CLIENT: New Performance Nutrition / DESIGNER: Jeffrey Bucholtz / ART DIRECTOR: Joel Templin, Katie Jain
**156:** COMPANY: Joseph Blalock Design Office / CLIENT: Braun & Butler Construction / DESIGNER: Joseph Blalock / ART DIRECTORS: Rex Peteet, Sibley/Peteet Design
**157:** COMPANY: Schwartzrock Graphic Arts / CLIENT: Kim Baker Communications / DESIGNER: Sherwin Schwartzrock
**158:** COMPANY: Schwartzrock Graphic Arts / CLIENT: Dennis Magner / DESIGNER: Sherwin Schwartzrock
**159:** COMPANY: Design Center, Inc. / CLIENT: Avonlea Floral Arts / DESIGNER: Sherwin Schwartzrock / ART DIRECTOR: John Reger
**160:** COMPANY: Hatch Design / CLIENT: Riggs Distributiong / DESIGNER: Nate Luetkehans / ART DIRECTORS: Joel Templin, Katie Jain

Eat.   Learn.   Live.

161

162

163

164

165

166

CHRISTIAN LIFE
MINISTRIES

*Bringing God's Word to Life*

167

168

**161:** COMPANY: Tactix Creative, Inc. / CLIENT: Chartwells Gumbo / DESIGNER: Paul Howalt
**162:** COMPANY: Felix Sockwell / CLIENT: U.S. Holocaust Memorial Museum / DESIGNERs: Felix Sockwell, Thomas Fuchs, Stephan Sagmeister, Robert Festino
**163:** COMPANY: Tactix Creative, Inc. / CLIENT: MD Bugs / DESIGNER: Paul Howalt
**164:** COMPANY: Schwartzrock Graphic Arts / CLIENT: Kingswood Camp & Retreat Ministries / DESIGNER: Sherwin Schwartzrock
**165:** COMPANY: Joseph Blalock Design Office / CLIENT: James Plant Racecars / DESIGNER: Joseph Blalock
**166:** COMPANY: Glischka Studios / CLIENT: Tesser / DESIGNER: Von Glitschka / ART DIRECTOR: Scott Gagner
**167:** COMPANY: Schwartzrock Graphic Arts / CLIENT: Christian Life Ministries / DESIGNER: Sherwin Schwartzrock
**168:** COMPANY: Glischka Studios / CLIENT: Gilbert House Publishing / DESIGNER: Von Glitschka / ART DIRECTOR: Von Glitschka

169

**Iowa Orthodontic Solutions**
We make **Iowasmile.com**

170

171

172

173

174

175

176

**169:** COMPANY: Schwartzrock Graphic Arts / CLIENT: Kingstone Media / DESIGNER: Sherwin Schwartzrock / ART DIRECTOR:
**170:** COMPANY: J Sayles Design Co. / CLIENT: Iowa Orthodontic Solutions / DESIGNER: John Sayles / ART DIRECTOR: John Sayles
**171:** CLIENT: Jennifer & Dwayne Dunnivan / DESIGNER: Mike Jones
**172:** COMPANY: Joseph Blalock Design Office / CLIENT: Green Horse Financial Consulting / DESIGNER: Joseph Blalock / ART DIRECTOR: Adam Dalch
**173:** COMPANY: Tactix Creative, Inc. / CLIENT: Louisiana Dental Care / DESIGNER: Paul Howalt
**174:** COMPANY: Tactix Creative, Inc. / CLIENT: Watts Gwilliam / DESIGNER: Paul Howalt
**175:** COMPANY: Schwartzrock Graphic Arts / CLIENT: Worlds of Wow / DESIGNER: Sherwin Schwartzrock
**176:** COMPANY: Joseph Blalock Design Office / CLIENT: Biz Stylist / DESIGNER: Joseph Blalock

# A Closer Look

**FIRM:** THE GRETEMAN GROUP
**DESIGNER / ILLUSTRATOR:** CHRIS PARKS
**ART DIRECTOR:** SONIA GRETEMAN
**WRITERS:** SONIA GRETEMAN / DEANNA HARMS
**CLIENT:** ANONYMOUS

A Kansas-based philanthropist, who prefers anonymity, set a goal of making Kansas the number one state in the country for volunteerism. At the time, Kansas ranked eighth. To reach number one, 150,000+ volunteers were needed. His foundation created a website to serve as a clearinghouse for volunteerism. Our challenge: To drive participation in a somewhat complicated program.

Our Come & Give It campaign delivers a strong call to action. Everything from posters to scout cards, billboards to TV spots, drive you to VolunteerKansas.org. A compelling animated video on the homepage inspires Kansans to roll up their sleeves and make a difference, improving the lives of their neighbors, and their communities. The campaign breaks down the ways to give —volunteer, microgrants, exchange—and tells you just enough to make you go to the website to learn more, and hopefully, take action.

Kansas hasn't yet reached its ambitious number one goal, but VolunteerKansas.org won't rest until it does. And it's showing progress. It's moved up a step to seventh!

*This logo is brilliant in so many ways. The clever twist in the language of the copy line alone inspires you to want to be a part of this movement.*

*The sophistication and vibrancy of the color palette used for the television spots captivates the viewer. It provides a beautifully moving backdrop for highlighting elements such as the giving of your heart and time to service, which are icons highlighted here in white.*

**COME&GIVEIT**

**3 WAYS TO COME & GIVE IT**

| **VOLUNTEER** | **MICROGRANTS** | **EXCHANGE** |
|---|---|---|
| Just visit the website. You can easily match your time and talents to a good cause. | A little bit makes a huge difference to somebody who needs a boost. | Online classifieds where people who have find organizations that need. |

**V** volunteerkansas.org

👁

*The multifaceted hand in the logo brilliantly speaks to the many ways each one of us can make a difference in our communities. The stars reflect the magically transformative nature of charity service in general.*

👁

*It's refreshing to see a completely graphic public service campaign. I suspect the success of this series of ads can be traced back to the gorgeously unexpected logo and graphic visual language surrounding it.*

177

178

179

180

182

181

183

**177:** COMPANY: Device / CLIENT: Death Ray magazine / DESIGNER: Rian Hughes / ART DIRECTOR: Rian Hughes
**178:** COMPANY: Jon Flaming Design / CLIENT: Pure Luck Farm & Dairy / DESIGNER: Jon Flaming / ART DIRECTOR: Jon Flaming
**179:** COMPANY: Tactix Creative, Inc. / CLIENT: Simplex Plumbing / DESIGNER: Paul Howalt
**180:** COMPANY: Device / CLIENT: Sterling Brands / DESIGNER: Rian Hughes / ART DIRECTOR: Crispin Reed
**181:** COMPANY: Tactix Creative, Inc. / CLIENT: Cross Roads Youth Group / DESIGNER: Paul Howalt
**182:** COMPANY: Tim Frame Design / CLIENT: LOOPS / DESIGNER: Tim Frame / ART DIRECTOR: Andrew Constantinides
**183:** COMPANY: Melodic Firtue / CLIENT: Tin Man Brewing Co. / DESIGNER: Aaron Tanner / ART DIRECTOR: Aaron Tanner

184

185

CHOICE MOTOR
*Credit*

186

187

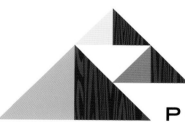 POCONO MODERN

188

189

190

184: COMPANY: Dotzero Design / CLIENT: The Big Float / DESIGNERS: Jon Wippich, Karen Wippich / ART DIRECTORS: Jon Wippich, Karen Wippich
185: COMPANY: Mattson Creative / CLIENT: Scott / DESIGNER: Ty Mattson
186: COMPANY: Tactix Creative, Inc. / CLIENT: Choice Motor Credit / DESIGNER: Paul Howalt
187: COMPANY: Tim Frame Design / CLIENT: American Bathtub Refinishers / DESIGNER: Tim Frame / ART DIRECTOR: Tim Frame
188: COMPANY: Mattson Creative / DESIGNER: Ty Mattson
189: COMPANY: leightonhubbell.com / CLIENT: / DESIGNER: Leighton Hubbell / ART DIRECTOR: Leighton Hubbell
190: COMPANY: Tactix Creative, Inc. / CLIENT: Stonebridge Manor / DESIGNER: Paul Howalt

191

192

193

194

195

196

197

198

**191:** COMPANY: Tim Frame Design / CLIENT: Towne Bakery / DESIGNER: Tim Frame / ART DIRECTOR: Jason Sigala
**192:** COMPANY: Glischka Studios / CLIENT: Barbara Vick Design / DESIGNER: Von Glitschka / ART DIRECTOR: Barbara Vick
**193:** COMPANY: Schwartzrock Graphic Arts / CLIENT: Acsent Marketing / DESIGNER: Sherwin Schwartzrock
**194:** COMPANY: Design Center, Inc. / DESIGNER: Sherwin Schwartzrock / ART DIRECTOR: John Reger
**195:** COMPANY: Schwartzrock Graphic Arts / CLIENT: Lamp Post Publishing / DESIGNER: Sherwin Schwartzrock
**196:** COMPANY: Schwartzrock Graphic Arts / CLIENT: Westwood Lutheran Church / DESIGNER: Sherwin Schwartzrock
**197:** COMPANY: Schwartzrock Graphic Arts / CLIENT: BI Worldwide / DESIGNER: Sherwin Schwartzrock
**198:** COMPANY: R&R Partners / CLIENT: Personal / DESIGNER: Randy Heil / ART DIRECTOR: Randy Heil

199

200

201

202

203

204

205

206

207

JBC
CONTENIMIENTO

208

209

210

24 blooms

211

MARTIN LUTHER ACADEMY

212

213

**207:** COMPANY: Schwartzrock Graphic Arts / CLIENT: Lure Design / DESIGNER: Sherwin Schwartzrock
**208:** COMPANY: Salvadore Anguiano / CLIENT: Jbc Containment / DESIGNER: Salvadore Anguiano / ART DIRECTOR: Salvadore Anguiano
**209:** COMPANY: Schwartzrock Graphic Arts / CLIENT: Design Center / DESIGNER: Sherwin Schwartzrock
**210:** COMPANY: Schwartzrock Graphic Arts / CLIENT: RiverBrand Design / DESIGNER: Sherwin Schwartzrock
**211:** COMPANY: Monique Maloney Design / CLIENT: 24 Blooms / DESIGNER: / ART DIRECTOR: Monique Maloney
**212:** COMPANY: Schwartzrock Graphic Arts / CLIENT: 3.2.1. Inc. / DESIGNER: Sherwin Schwartzrock
**213:** COMPANY: Device / CLIENT: Dilemma / DESIGNER: Rian Hughes / ART DIRECTOR: J.C. Christofilis

SkillKites

214

ILENT FILM

215

216

217

218

219

214: COMPANY: leightonhubbell.com / CLIENT: Skill Kites / DESIGNER: Leighton Hubbell / ART DIRECTOR: Leighton Hubbell
215: CLIENT: Retail / Real Estate / DESIGNER: Chris Parks / ART DIRECTOR: Chris Parks
216: COMPANY: Schwartzrock Graphic Arts / CLIENT: RiverBrand Design / DESIGNER: Sherwin Schwartzrock
217: COMPANY: Device / CLIENT: Bieler Bros Music / DESIGNER: Rian Hughes / ART DIRECTOR: Rian Hughes
218: COMPANY: Schwartzrock Graphic Arts / CLIENT: City of Winsted / DESIGNER: Sherwin Schwartzrock
219: COMPANY: Schwartzrock Graphic Arts / CLIENT: RiverBrand Design / DESIGNER: Sherwin Schwartzrock

220

221

222

223

224

225

226

227

**220:** COMPANY: Schwartzrock Graphic Arts / CLIENT: RiverBrand Design / DESIGNER: Sherwin Schwartzrock
**221:** COMPANY: Design Center, Inc. / CLIENT: Root River Trail Association / DESIGNER: Sherwin Schwartzrock / ART DIRECTOR: John Reger
**222:** COMPANY: Schwartzrock Graphic Arts / CLIENT: Design Center / DESIGNER: Sherwin Schwartzrock
**223:** COMPANY: Sean Heisler / CLIENT: FanMix / DESIGNER: Sean Heisler / ART DIRECTOR: Sean Heisler
**224:** COMPANY: Schwartzrock Graphic Arts / CLIENT: Kingstone Media / DESIGNER: Sherwin Schwartzrock / ART DIRECTOR:
**225:** COMPANY: Sean Heisler / CLIENT: BBQ Notes / DESIGNER: Sean Heisler / ART DIRECTOR: Sean Heisler
**226:** COMPANY: Schwartzrock Graphic Arts / CLIENT: Freshwater Church / DESIGNER: Sherwin Schwartzrock
**227:** COMPANY: Design Center, Inc. / CLIENT: Aquapex / DESIGNER: Sherwin Schwartzrock / ART DIRECTOR: John Reger

228

**Rejoicing Partners**

229

230

MyPitbullisFamily.org

231

CAESAR

232

233

BLACKWOOD

MANAGEMENT GROUP

234

235

**228:** COMPANY: Schwartzrock Graphic Arts / CLIENT: Blackwood Management Group / DESIGNER: Sherwin Schwartzrock
**229:** COMPANY: Schwartzrock Graphic Arts / CLIENT: St. Philip the Deacon Lutheran Church / DESIGNER: Sherwin Schwartzrock
**230:** CLIENT: Todd Sullens / DESIGNER: Mike Jones
**231:** COMPANY: Schwartzrock Graphic Arts / CLIENT: Yanovick, Inc. / DESIGNER: Sherwin Schwartzrock
**232:** COMPANY: Schwartzrock Graphic Arts / CLIENT: Kingstone Media / DESIGNER: Sherwin Schwartzrock
**233:** COMPANY: Schwartzrock Graphic Arts / CLIENT: Lamp Post Publishing / DESIGNER: Sherwin Schwartzrock
**234:** COMPANY: Schwartzrock Graphic Arts / CLIENT: Blackwood Management Group / DESIGNER: Sherwin Schwartzrock
**235:** CLIENT: Todd & Storey Reaves / DESIGNER: Mike Jones

**FIRM:** TIM FRAME DESIGN
**DESIGNER / ILLUSTRATOR:** TIM FRAME
**CLIENT:** REDCAST

I was asked to do an identity project encompassing logo development and additional graphic components to be used for stickers and other band promotions.

The client, Redcast, is a few guys from Portland, Oregon, trying to brighten peoples' day with a little bit of retro-pop sunshine. The band is made up of three brothers: Jarrod, Seth, and Darren Brock, who grew up listening to the oldies station, and it shows. They've somehow fused their '60s rock 'n' roll influence with alt-rock sensibilities, and created something that sounds like The Format went on a date with Hellogoodbye and then got mugged by Jet. Redcast has no Billboard-topping aspirations or delusions of grandeur—they just want to play their retro brand of indie pop music and make people smile. Their first full-length album *Talent Show Runners Up* was released in 2011.

Art direction from the client read as follows: We want the Redcast logo to be old and new at the same time—retro but current, familiar but still fresh. It should look the way our music sounds. Above everything else, it needs to be fun. Visually, we tend to draw inspiration from vintage advertisements and lo-fi photography.

*Good band logos are sometimes a difficult sell with so many strong artistic personalities in the room. One way to combat the focus of critiquing a logo to death is to create an entire set of eight fully formed interchangeable and complementary marks. It takes the focus off of just one logo needing to represent the group.*

*These bold graphic beauties are reducible, retro, red, rockin', and right on target. I can visualize each one as a tattoo on my upper arm.*

With so much visual excitement, hard-hitting impact, and perfectly crafted line weight ratios, it's easy to forget that they are all one-color marks.

The main logo, here applied to a red Stratocaster, radiates from a very fortunate placement of the letter C in the name. The sound waves also can be seen as track lines on an old vinyl LP. Yeah, that's right, I said LP... Look it up.

236

237

239

238

240

CONSTRUCTIVE
CHAOS

241

242

**236:** COMPANY: Art Chantry Design / CLIENT: Verve Records / DESIGNER: Art Chantry / ART DIRECTOR: Art Chantry
**237:** COMPANY: Chase Design Group / CLIENT: EcoAmerica / DESIGNER: Jinny Bae / ART DIRECTORS: Margo Chase, Jinny Bae
**238:** COMPANY: REACTOR design Studio / CLIENT: KVC / DESIGNER: Chase Wilson, Micah Barta / ART DIRECTOR: Clifton Alexander
**239:** COMPANY: Spindletop Design / CLIENT: Amaya Roadsting Co. / DESIGNERS: Jennifer Blanco, Laura Tait, Tyler Swanner / ART DIRECTOR: Jennifer Blanco
**240:** COMPANY: Sean Heisler / CLIENT: BarCode / DESIGNER: Sean Heisler / ART DIRECTOR: Sean Heisler
**241:** COMPANY: Rule29 / CLIENT: Constructive Chaos / DESIGNER: Suson Herda / ART DIRECTOR: Justin Ahrens
**242:** COMPANY: Jon Flaming Design / CLIENT: KERA/Dallas / DESIGNER: Jon Flaming / ART DIRECTOR: Jon Flaming

243

244

245

246

Modern Medical

247

248

249

**243:** COMPANY: Tim Frame Design / CLIENT: Upper Arlinton Community HS / DESIGNER: Tim Frame / ART DIRECTOR: Melissa Hasebrook
**244:** COMPANY: Duct Tape & Glitter / CLIENT: Render Hog / DESIGNER: Luke Bott
**245:** COMPANY: U! Creative, Inc. / CLIENT: May Microphones & Marching Percussions International / DESIGNER: U! Creative Team
**246:** CLIENT: Entertainment / DESIGNER: Chris Parks / ART DIRECTOR: Chris Parks
**247:** COMPANY: Jeremy Slagle Graphic Design / CLIENT: Modern Medical / DESIGNER: Jeremy Slagle / ART DIRECTOR: Jeremy Slagle
**248:** COMPANY: Tim Frame Design / CLIENT: Carolina Technology Alliance / DESIGNER: Tim Frame / ART DIRECTOR: John Walker
**249:** COMPANY: Weather Control / CLIENT: Seattle ADDYS / DESIGNER: Josh Oakley

250

251

252

253

254

255

256

257

**250:** CLIENT: Nike / DESIGNER: Mike Calkins
**251:** COMPANY: Schwartzrock Graphic Arts / CLIENT: RiverBrand Design / DESIGNER: Sherwin Schwartzrock
**252:** COMPANY: Schwartzrock Graphic Arts / CLIENT: Eason and Associates / DESIGNER: Sherwin Schwartzrock / ART DIRECTOR: Brad Latham
**253:** COMPANY: Schwartzrock Graphic Arts / CLIENT: Tami Herndon / DESIGNER: Sherwin Schwartzrock
**254:** COMPANY: Jeremy Slagle Graphic Design / CLIENT: Maximin Project / DESIGNER: Jeremy Slagle / ART DIRECTOR: Jeremy Slagle
**255:** COMPANY: Design Center, Inc. / CLIENT: Rightway Auto Glass / DESIGNER: Sherwin Schwartzrock / ART DIRECTOR: Ken Haus
**256:** COMPANY: Design Center, Inc. / CLIENT: DSI / DESIGNER: Sherwin Schwartzrock / ART DIRECTOR: John Reger
**257:** COMPANY: Design Center, Inc. / CLIENT: DSI / DESIGNER: Sherwin Schwartzrock / ART DIRECTOR: John Reger

SILVERLANE

258

259

260

261

262

263

264

265

**258:** COMPANY: Tactix Creative, Inc. / CLIENT: Silverlane Estates / DESIGNER: Paul Howalt
**259:** COMPANY: Schwartzrock Graphic Arts / CLIENT: Target / DESIGNER: Sherwin Schwartzrock
**260:** COMPANY: Schwartzrock Graphic Arts / CLIENT: Freshwater Church / DESIGNER: Sherwin Schwartzrock
**261:** COMPANY: Charpentier Hovland Advertising / CLIENT: SportsBook / DESIGNER: Sherwin Schwartzrock / ART DIRECTOR: Shannon Charpentier
**262:** COMPANY: Matt Lehman Studio / CLIENT: Convoy of Hope (via Penguin Creative) / ART DIRECTOR: Lee Steffen
**263:** COMPANY: Schwartzrock Graphic Arts / CLIENT: Design Center / DESIGNER: Sherwin Schwartzrock
**264:** COMPANY: Design Center, Inc. / CLIENT: Byerly's and Lunds / DESIGNER: Sherwin Schwartzrock / ART DIRECTOR: John Reger
**265:** COMPANY: Design Center, Inc. / CLIENT: 401k Latte / DESIGNER: Sherwin Schwartzrock / ART DIRECTOR: John Reger

266

267

268

269

270

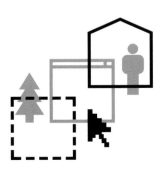

271

272

266: COMPANY: Adam Anderson / DESIGNER: Adam Anderson
267: COMPANY: Schwartzrock Graphic Arts / CLIENT: Nazarene Publishing House / DESIGNER: Sherwin Schwartzrock
268: COMPANY: Schwartzrock Graphic Arts / CLIENT: Precision Product Design, Inc. / DESIGNER: Sherwin Schwartzrock
269: COMPANY: Schwartzrock Graphic Arts / CLIENT: Pugleasa Company / DESIGNER: Sherwin Schwartzrock
270: COMPANY: Schwartzrock Graphic Arts / CLIENT: Herman Miller / DESIGNER: Sherwin Schwartzrock
271: COMPANY: Design Center, Inc. / CLIENT: Design Center / DESIGNER: Sherwin Schwartzrock / ART DIRECTOR: John Reger
272: COMPANY: Schwartzrock Graphic Arts / CLIENT: BI Worldwide / DESIGNER: Sherwin Schwartzrock

# 1OO HOCKADAY

*Celebrate. Imagine.*

273

274

276

PLAYERS
SPORT · CLUB
AT TREETOPS

275

277

278

**273:** COMPANY: Banowetz & Company / CLIENT: The Hockaday School / DESIGNER: Lily Smith+Kirkley / ART DIRECTOR: Eric Venegas
**274:** COMPANY: Schwartzrock Graphic Arts / CLIENT: Vanessa Martinson / DESIGNER: Sherwin Schwartzrock
**275:** COMPANY: Schwartzrock Graphic Arts / CLIENT: Enhanced Landscaping / DESIGNER: Sherwin Schwartzrock
**276:** COMPANY: Schwartzrock Graphic Arts / CLIENT: RiverBrand Design / DESIGNER: Sherwin Schwartzrock
**277:** COMPANY: Schwartzrock Graphic Arts / CLIENT: MN Health and Housing Association / DESIGNER: Sherwin Schwartzrock
**278:** COMPANY: Schwartzrock Graphic Arts / CLIENT: T. Cook / DESIGNER: Sherwin Schwartzrock

# Logo Gallery

279

280

281

282

283

284

285

286

**279:** COMPANY: Design Center, Inc. / CLIENT: Design Center / DESIGNER: Sherwin Schwartzrock / ART DIRECTOR: John Reger
**280:** COMPANY: Schwartzrock Graphic Arts / CLIENT: St. Philip the Deacon Lutheran Church / DESIGNER: Sherwin Schwartzrock
**281:** COMPANY: Design Center, Inc. / CLIENT: Oak Technology / DESIGNER: Sherwin Schwartzrock / ART DIRECTOR: John Reger
**282:** COMPANY: chameleon design / CLIENT: Peter Varga / DESIGNER: Tomas Vateha / ART DIRECTOR: Tomas Vateha
**282:** COMPANY: Schwartzrock Graphic Arts / CLIENT: Target / DESIGNER: Sherwin Schwartzrock
**284:** COMPANY: Schwartzrock Graphic Arts / CLIENT: BI Worldwide / DESIGNER: Sherwin Schwartzrock
**285:** COMPANY: Schwartzrock Graphic Arts / CLIENT: Initio3i / DESIGNER: Sherwin Schwartzrock
**286:** COMPANY: Design Center, Inc. / CLIENT: American Asset Management / DESIGNER: Sherwin Schwartzrock / ART DIRECTOR: John Reger

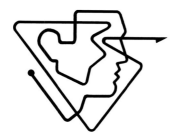

287

288

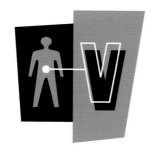

289

290

291

292

293

294

**287:** COMPANY: Design Center, Inc. / CLIENT: Design Center / DESIGNER: Sherwin Schwartzrock / ART DIRECTOR: John Reger
**288:** COMPANY: Schwartzrock Graphic Arts / CLIENT: Target / DESIGNER: Sherwin Schwartzrock
**289:** COMPANY: Schwartzrock Graphic Arts / CLIENT: Yanovick, Inc. / DESIGNER: Sherwin Schwartzrock
**290:** COMPANY: Design Center, Inc. / CLIENT: Pink Interiors / DESIGNER: Sherwin Schwartzrock / ART DIRECTOR: John Reger
**291:** COMPANY: Schwartzrock Graphic Arts / CLIENT: Kingstone Media / DESIGNER: Sherwin Schwartzrock
**292:** COMPANY: Schwartzrock Graphic Arts / CLIENT: Kingstone Media / DESIGNER: Sherwin Schwartzrock
**293:** COMPANY: Charpentier Hovland Advertising / CLIENT: Lake Region Elect. Coop. / DESIGNER: Sherwin Schwartzrock / ART DIRECTOR: Shannon Charopentier
**294:** COMPANY: Schwartzrock Graphic Arts / CLIENT: Schwartzrock Graphic Arts / DESIGNER: Sherwin Schwartzrock

# Meaning

ALINA WHEELER

As countries, corporations, and communities leverage their brands to gain a transcendent advantage in the global marketplace, it is more important than ever to rise above the competitive clamor. To be memorable and dramatically differentiated is quite simply survival. As the world migrates to the mobile, the role of the logo is more important than ever. The best logos swiftly unlock a series of associations that reinforce the emotional connection to a brand.

Following are seven principles about the vital relationship between logos and meaning.

**1. Logos are vessels for meaning.**
The best logos stand for something and have meaning that is nurtured over time. Milton Glaser said it best, "The logo is the gateway to the brand." When you see a logo, it should swiftly unlock a series of associations that are built over time. Many decision makers could benefit from this simple truth. Logos and visual symbols are the fastest communication on earth. Like the flag of a nation, a logo should communicate who you are and what you stand for.

**2. Key decision makers should agree on what the brand stands for prior to seeing any design solutions.**
What the brand stands for and "we know who we are" is the foundation of building a brand. It is hard work whether the brand builder is a start-up or revitalizing an existing brand—and whether the work is evolutionary or revolutionary. Designers have a great capacity to distill vast amounts of information, and should work with their clients to create a simple one-page 11 x 17 (27.9 x 43.2 cm) brand brief that synthesizes the big idea, the competitive advantage, the value proposition, the target market, marketplace insights and trends, brand attributes, key offerings, and key competitors. We have all been to presentations where a decision maker looks at a design, and says, "That is not who we are." Focus first on "who we are." A brand brief is a sustainable and valuable tool.

*a*  *b*  *c*  *d*

### 3. Meaning is rarely immediate. Meaning is assigned, and evolves over time.

When the Nike logo was designed in 1971 by Carolyn Davidson (fig a), it was an abstraction of the wing of the Greek goddess of victory. Its current top-of-mind association is "Just do it." The symbol stands for something that is deep and profound to its customers. Frequent and consistent exposure integrated the symbol and its meaning into popular culture. The three-pointed star of Mercedes Benz (fig b) was designed in 1886 to symbolize Daimler's ambition of universal motorization "on land, on water and in the air." More than a century later, it stands for luxury and performance that is demonstrated through their product design and meticulous engineering.

### 4. Meaning is the best catalyst for the design process.

When a designer lives inside of the big idea, they have an opportunity to use their talent to fuse visual form with brand intelligence. Coupled with insights about the target audience, competitive and best-practice audits, the designer can achieve remarkable results that will be sustainable. The great thing about being a designer is that you can show what the future could look like and spark meaningful discussions about the brand.

### 5. Every opportunity and touchpoint to reinforce and demonstrate the link between the logo and what the brand stands for should be seized.

During the process, each design presentation should begin with the big idea and then demonstrate how the logo, look and feel, core typefaces, color palette, and other brand elements express the big idea. Make meaning the campfire for decision makers. A logo should always be shown in context of a real application so that it appears real. When the logo is launched, the organization needs to communicate what the brand stands for. The standards need to begin with that, and not just clarify usage guidelines.

### 6. Logos become recognizable when they are used consistently and frequently across touchpoints.

The logo should be viewed as a brand asset that symbolizes what the brand stands for. Even in the tiniest organizations, the logo is seen thousands and thousands of times. It is important to make it easy to adhere to standards—the logo is a workhorse. Designing a logo and then not having standards is a huge waste. The logo and the look and feel are brand assets that need to be managed and protected. The best consumer brands benefit from frequency and consistency. Logos like Target (fig c), Starbucks (fig d), and Nike (fig a) no longer need a logotype. Why? Because the brain sees shapes first, and then reads text.

### 7. No one does it alone.

Businesses do not succeed because they have a great logo. They succeed because they stand for something, and create something that is relevant and needed. They deliver on their promise and know what their promise is. They succeed because they are relentless in their quest to be the brand of choice. It is not your logo; it is their logo. It is not your brand; it is your client's brand. Building trust and listening carefully to the client and to the marketplace is what the best designers do, in addition to being the best designers they can be.

People fall in love with brands that they cannot imagine living without. A logo and how it lives across platforms is a tangible expression that sparks associations of the brand for all the stakeholders. Designers are the professionals that distill meaning and make it easy for people to emotionally connect, navigate, and make choices.

295

296

297

298

299

300

301

**295:** COMPANY: Sean Heisler / CLIENT: Studio You Portraits / DESIGNER: Sean Heisler / ART DIRECTOR: Sean Heisler
**296:** COMPANY: Chase Design Group / CLIENT: LAAC - IAC Aerobatic Chapter / DESIGNER: Margo Chase / ART DIRECTOR: Margo Chase
**297:** COMPANY: TY Design / CLIENT: Vitis / DESIGNER: Ty Wilkins / ART DIRECTOR: Ed Nacional
**298:** CLIENT: Baseline Creative / DESIGNER: Chris Parks / ART DIRECTOR: Nathan Williams
**299:** COMPANY: Entermotion / CLIENT: Jubilation Event Planners / DESIGNER: Lea Morrow / ART DIRECTOR: Joe Morrow
**300:** COMPANY: Mission-MInded / CLIENT: Education Outside / DESIGNER: Clint G. Delapaz / ART DIRECTOR: Rod Lemaire
**301:** COMPANY: DesignUnion / CLIENT: Rockford Aquarium / DESIGNER: Renee Melton

302

303

304

305

306

307

308

302: COMPANY: Phelps / CLIENT: Aiya America, Inc. / DESIGNER: Collateral design: Zareh Ter-Stapanian / ART DIRECTOR: Identity Design: Hiroko Suyama
303: COMPANY: Plazma Design / CLIENT: Mollie Day Imports / DESIGNER: Todd Hansson / ART DIRECTOR: Todd Hansson
304: COMPANY: Schwartzrock Graphic Arts / CLIENT: Noram, Inc. / DESIGNER: Sherwin Schwartzrock
305: COMPANY: Pacey + Pacey Design / CLIENT: The Control Group / DESIGNER: Michael Pacey / ART DIRECTOR: Robert Pacey
306: COMPANY: Banowetz & Company / CLIENT: Pro Soap / DESIGNER: Eric Venegas / ART DIRECTOR: Eric Venegas
307: COMPANY: Device / CLIENT: DC Comics / DESIGNER: Rian Hughes / ART DIRECTOR: Kenny Lopez
308: COMPANY: Tim Frame Design / CLIENT: TIP TOP Bake Shop / DESIGNER: Tim Frame / ART DIRECTOR: Lauren Reece

309

310

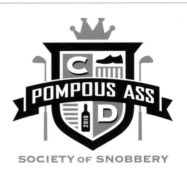

311

312

313

314

315

316

**309:** COMPANY: Invisible Creature / CLIENT: Reach Records / DESIGNER: Don Clark / ART DIRECTOR: Don Clark
**310:** COMPANY: Design Center, Inc. / CLIENT: Design Center / DESIGNER: Sherwin Schwartzrock / ART DIRECTOR: John Reger
**311:** COMPANY: Schwartzrock Graphic Arts / CLIENT: Freshwater Church / DESIGNER: Sherwin Schwartzrock
**312:** COMPANY: R&R Partners / CLIENT: Arnie DiGeorge / DESIGNER: Randy Heil / ART DIRECTOR: Randy Heil
**313:** COMPANY: Schwartzrock Graphic Arts / CLIENT: 3.2.1. Inc. / DESIGNER: Sherwin Schwartzrock
**314:** COMPANY: Schwartzrock Graphic Arts / CLIENT: MJ Sund / DESIGNER: Sherwin Schwartzrock
**315:** COMPANY: Schwartzrock Graphic Arts / CLIENT: BI Worldwide / DESIGNER: Sherwin Schwartzrock
**316:** COMPANY: Schwartzrock Graphic Arts / CLIENT: Medtronic / DESIGNER: Sherwin Schwartzrock

317

318

319

320

321

322

323

324

317: COMPANY: Sean Heisler / CLIENT: Urban Gourmet / DESIGNER: Sean Heisler / ART DIRECTOR: Sean Heisler
318: COMPANY: Invisible Creature / CLIENT: The Service Station / DESIGNER: Ryan Clark / ART DIRECTOR: Ryan Clark
319: COMPANY: TY Design / CLIENT: Cloudup / DESIGNER: Ty Wilkins / ART DIRECTOR: Ty Wilkins
320: COMPANY: Schwartzrock Graphic Arts / CLIENT: Wiese Creative / DESIGNER: Sherwin Schwartzrock
321: COMPANY: Schwartzrock Graphic Arts / CLIENT: American Bible Society / DESIGNER: Sherwin Schwartzrock
322: COMPANY: Tim Frame Design / CLIENT: Rightway Media / DESIGNER: Tim Frame / ART DIRECTOR: Alex Perry
323: COMPANY: Schwartzrock Graphic Arts / CLIENT: MHHA / DESIGNER: Sherwin Schwartzrock / ART DIRECTOR: Sherwin Schwartzrock
324: COMPANY: Schwartzrock Graphic Arts / CLIENT: 3.2.1. Inc. / DESIGNER: Sherwin Schwartzrock

325

**WESTWOOD**
LUTHERAN CHURCH

326

327

328

329

330

**METRON**
PRESS

331

DESIGN

332

333

334

335

336

337

**332:** COMPANY: DesignUnion / CLIENT: DesignUnion / DESIGNER: Renee Melton
**333:** COMPANY: Schwartzrock Graphic Arts / CLIENT: Community Comics / DESIGNER: Sherwin Schwartzrock
**334:** COMPANY: Owen Jones Design / CLIENT: AYR / Personal Finance & Utilities / DESIGNER: Owen Jones / ART DIRECTOR: Owen Jones
**335:** COMPANY: Invisible Creature / CLIENT: Wiseguys Entertainment / DESIGNER: Ryan Clark / ART DIRECTOR: Ryan Clark
**336:** COMPANY: Schwartzrock Graphic Arts / CLIENT: BI Worldwide / DESIGNER: Sherwin Schwartzrock
**337:** COMPANY: Schwartzrock Graphic Arts / CLIENT: Design Center / DESIGNER: Sherwin Schwartzrock

338

339

340

341

WINSOME
WOODS

342

343

344

345

**338:** COMPANY: Schwartzrock Graphic Arts / CLIENT: Freshwater Church / DESIGNER: Sherwin Schwartzrock
**339:** COMPANY: Design Center, Inc. / CLIENT: Target / DESIGNER: Sherwin Schwartzrock / ART DIRECTOR: John Reger
**340:** COMPANY: BellBoy Creative / CLIENT: Feeding Without Frenzy / DESIGNER: Noah Bell / ART DIRECTOR: Noah Bell
**341:** COMPANY: Schwartzrock Graphic Arts / CLIENT: Herman Miller / DESIGNER: Sherwin Schwartzrock
**342:** COMPANY: Schwartzrock Graphic Arts / CLIENT: RiverBrand Design / DESIGNER: Sherwin Schwartzrock
**343:** COMPANY: Fernandez Studio / CLIENT: SIMA Financial Group / DESIGNER: Carlos Fernandez / ART DIRECTOR: Mark Smith
**344:** COMPANY: Schwartzrock Graphic Arts / CLIENT: Wiese Communications / DESIGNER: Sherwin Schwartzrock
**345:** COMPANY: Design Center, Inc. / CLIENT: Design Center / DESIGNER: Sherwin Schwartzrock / ART DIRECTOR: John Reger

346

347

348

349

350

351

352

353

**346:** COMPANY: Schwartzrock Graphic Arts / CLIENT: 3i. Inc. / DESIGNER: Sherwin Schwartzrock
**347:** COMPANY: Schwartzrock Graphic Arts / CLIENT: BI Worldwide / DESIGNER: Sherwin Schwartzrock
**348:** COMPANY: Design Center, Inc. / CLIENT: 401k Latte / DESIGNER: Sherwin Schwartzrock / ART DIRECTOR: John Reger
**349:** COMPANY: Gardner Design / CLIENT: Bluebird Books / DESIGNER: Brian Miller / ART DIRECTOR: Brian Miller
**350:** COMPANY: Schwartzrock Graphic Arts / CLIENT: Kingstone Media / DESIGNER: Sherwin Schwartzrock
**351:** COMPANY: Schwartzrock Graphic Arts / CLIENT: Wisdom Games / DESIGNER: Sherwin Schwartzrock
**352:** COMPANY: Schwartzrock Graphic Arts / CLIENT: Apparel Tiger / DESIGNER: Sherwin Schwartzrock
**353:** COMPANY: Schwartzrock Graphic Arts / CLIENT: Erica Allen / DESIGNER: Sherwin Schwartzrock

# A Closer Look

**FIRM:** HATCH
**DESIGNER / ILLUSTRATOR:** JEFFRY BUCHOLTZ
**ART DIRECTORS:** JOEL TEMPLIN / KATIE JAIN
**WRITER:** VINNIE CHIECO
**CLIENT:** NIK SOFTWARE

Nik Software is a company held in high esteem by professional photographers who use their photography software. They wanted to provide similarly intelligent tools to consumers and developed a platform-agnostic software product that makes it easier than ever for nonprofessionals to get greater quality and enjoyment out of their photos.

After months of collaboration with Nik marketing executives and lawyers, "Snapseed" was born. The name champions the view that every photo can be the beginning of something beautiful. With a little tending, it can grow into a greeting card, a slideshow, or a poster. We also developed the tagline, "Snap it. Tweak it. Love it. Share it." We then designed the logo, brand guidelines, and packaging.

*One of my favorite details of this logo is how the stroke width of the logotype directly relates to the width of the white borders of the photos on the mark.*

*The final Snapseed logo gives us a flower built from photos. It is also a visual metaphor of an SLR camera's leaf aperture mechanism.*

The naming process appeared to be quite thorough from the set of photos I received. Every potential app name pinned to the walls was solid. Snapseed, the final name chosen, evoked a definitive set of visual cues that were brilliantly explored.

This logo succeeds living in many environments. It was primarily designed to work well as an app icon on mobile devices, but you can see here how well it translates blown up large on a poster. Actual photos are inserted into the petals, which function as frames. The viewer is also rewarded with a brilliant tagline when they move in closer for the next level of details on the piece.

354

355

356

357

358

359

360

354: COMPANY: Art Chantry Design / CLIENT: Dave Crider, Estrus Records / DESIGNER: Art Chantry / ART DIRECTOR: Art Chantry
355: COMPANY: Gardner Design / CLIENT: Hustler Mowers / DESIGNER: Brian Miller / ART DIRECTOR: Brian Miller
356: COMPANY: Throttle Design Mechanics / CLIENT: CJ s Hot Rod Shop / DESIGNER: Sam Sedor / ART DIRECTOR: Dave Adamson
357: COMPANY: Dotzero Design / CLIENT: The Big Float / DESIGNERS: Jon Wippich, Karen Wippich / ART DIRECTORS: Jon Wippich, Karen Wippich
358: COMPANY: Michael Spitz Design / CLIENT: Michael Spitz Design / DESIGNER: Michael Spitz / ART DIRECTOR: Michael Spitz
359: COMPANY: Dotzero Design / CLIENT: Kate Sokoloff Creative / DESIGNERS: Jon Wippich, Karen Wippich / ART DIRECTORS: Jon Wippich, Karen Wippich
360: COMPANY: Pacey + Pacey Design / CLIENT: Boutique Roofer / DESIGNER: Michael Pacey / ART DIRECTOR: Robert Pacey

361

362

363

364

WorktoDate

365

366

367

361: COMPANY: Tim Frame Design / CLIENT: Tim Frame Design / DESIGNER: Tim Frame / ART DIRECTOR: Tim Frame
362: CLIENT: Guardian1 / DESIGNER: U! Creative Team
363: CLIENT: The Blairing Our with Eric Blair Show / DESIGNER: U! Creative Team
364: CLIENT: The Fall of Vegas / DESIGNER: U! Creative Team
365: COMPANY: WORKtoDATE (www.worktodate.com) / CLIENT: WORKtoDATE / DESIGNER: Greg Bennett / ART DIRECTOR: Greg Bennett
366: COMPANY: Throttle Design Mechanics / CLIENT: Ron Heagy / DESIGNER: Wendel Hayes / ART DIRECTOR: Dave Adamson
367: COMPANY: Dotzero Design / CLIENT: Live Wire Radio / DESIGNERS: Jon Wippich, Karen Wippich / ART DIRECTORS: Jon Wippich, Karen Wippich

368

369

370

371

372

373

374

375

**368:** COMPANY: Tim Frame Design / CLIENT: Tim Frame Design / DESIGNER: Tim Frame / ART DIRECTOR: Tim Frame
**369:** COMPANY: Schwartzrock Graphic Arts / CLIENT: BI Worldwide / DESIGNER: Sherwin Schwartzrock
**370:** COMPANY: R&R Partners / CLIENT: Personal / DESIGNER: Randy Heil / ART DIRECTOR: Randy Heil
**371:** COMPANY: Weather Control / CLIENT: Eye Can Art / DESIGNER: Josh Oakley
**372:** COMPANY: Schwartzrock Graphic Arts / CLIENT: BI Worldwide / DESIGNER: Sherwin Schwartzrock
**373:** COMPANY: R&R Partners / CLIENT: Utah Tobacco Prevention & Control / DESIGNER: Randy Heil / ART DIRECTOR: Randy Heil
**374:** COMPANY: R&R Partners / CLIENT: Harrah's Entertainment / DESIGNER: Randy Heil / ART DIRECTOR: Randy Heil
**375:** COMPANY: R&R Partners / CLIENT: Personal / DESIGNER: Randy Heil / ART DIRECTOR: Randy Heil

376

377

MOSAIC

378

**BELLE PLAINE**
ANIMAL HOSPITAL

379

380

381

382

383

376: COMPANY: Invisible Creature / CLIENT: Animal Media Group / DESIGNER: Ryan Clark / ART DIRECTOR: Ryan Clark
377: COMPANY: Schwartzrock Graphic Arts / CLIENT: Target / DESIGNER: Sherwin Schwartzrock
378: COMPANY: Schwartzrock Graphic Arts / CLIENT: 3.2.1. Inc / DESIGNER: Sherwin Schwartzrock
379: COMPANY: Design Center, Inc. / CLIENT: Belle Plaine Animal Hospital / DESIGNER: Sherwin Schwartzrock / ART DIRECTOR: John Reger
380: COMPANY: Flight Deck Creative / CLIENT: Dale Munson / DESIGNER: Jason Rahn / ART DIRECTOR: Jason Rahn
381: COMPANY: Flight Deck Creative / CLIENT: Mark Voss / DESIGNER: Jason Rahn / ART DIRECTOR: Jason Rahn
382: COMPANY: Schwartzrock Graphic Arts / CLIENT: Design Center / DESIGNER: Sherwin Schwartzrock
383: COMPANY: Schwartzrock Graphic Arts / CLIENT: Freshwater Church / DESIGNER: Sherwin Schwartzrock

**GUS-TRANS**

*Mit Erfahrung nach Osten*

385

IMPERIAL LAGER

384

386

387

388

**TorqueTec**

389

390

384: COMPANY: Mint / CLIENT: Hilliards Brewery / DESIGNER: Bryan Danknich / ART DIRECTOR: Mike Calkins
385: COMPANY: Floris Voorveld / CLIENT: G.U.S.-Trans / DESIGNER: Floris Voorveld
386: COMPANY: Schwartzrock Graphic Arts / CLIENT: Design Center / DESIGNER: Sherwin Schwartzrock
387: COMPANY: Schwartzrock Graphic Arts / CLIENT: BI Worldwide / DESIGNER: Sherwin Schwartzrock
388: COMPANY: Schwartzrock Graphic Arts / CLIENT: BI Worldwide / DESIGNER: Sherwin Schwartzrock
389: COMPANY: Schwartzrock Graphic Arts / CLIENT: TorqueTec / DESIGNER: Sherwin Schwartzrock
390: COMPANY: Schwartzrock Graphic Arts / CLIENT: Nazarene Publishing House / DESIGNER: Sherwin Schwartzrock

CALIFORNIA ASIAN EATERY

URBAN PICNIC

391

tcg ˢᴹ THE CREATIVE GROUP®

392

KRAVE®
JERKY

393

RIGHT WAY

AUTO GLASS

395

TAP

394

MOSAIC

396

391: COMPANY: Mode Design / CLIENT: Trang Nguyen / DESIGNER: Hans Bennewitz / ART DIRECTORS: Sage Smith, Hans Bennewitz
392: COMPANY: Hatch Design / CLIENT: Robert Half International / DESIGNER: Eszter Clark / ART DIRECTORS: Joel Templin, Katie Jain
393: COMPANY: Hatch Design / CLIENT: Krave Pure Easts, Inc. / DESIGNER: Will Ecke / ART DIRECTORS: Joel Templin, Katie Jain
394: COMPANY: leightonhubbell.com / CLIENT: Port of Long Beach / DESIGNER: Leighton Hubbell / ART DIRECTOR: Leighton Hubbell
395: COMPANY: Schwartzrock Graphic Arts / CLIENT: Design Center / DESIGNER: Sherwin Schwartzrock
396: COMPANY: Schwartzrock Graphic Arts / CLIENT: 3.2.1, Inc. / DESIGNER: Sherwin Schwartzrock

397

398

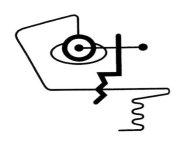

399

400

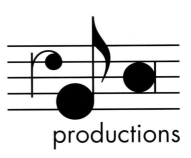

productions

401

402

403

404

**397:** COMPANY: Scwartzrock Grapic Arts / DESIGNER: Sherwin Schwartzrock
**398:** COMPANY: Schwartzrock Graphic Arts / CLIENT: Target / DESIGNER: Sherwin Schwartzrock
**399:** COMPANY: Design Center, Inc. / CLIENT: Design Center / DESIGNER: Sherwin Schwartzrock / ART DIRECTOR: John Reger
**400:** COMPANY: Little / CLIENT: Dick's Sporting Goods / DESIGNER: Santiago Crespo / ART DIRECTOR: Santiago Crespo
**401:** COMPANY: Pollard Design / DESIGNER: Jeff Pollard / ART DIRECTOR:
**402:** COMPANY: Schwartzrock Graphic Arts / CLIENT: RDA Productions / DESIGNER: Sherwin Schwartzrock
**403:** COMPANY: Matt Lehman Studio / CLIENT: General Mills (via Zeus Jones) / ART DIRECTOR: Brad Surcey
**404:** COMPANY: Schwartzrock Graphic Arts / CLIENT: RiverBrand Design / DESIGNER: Sherwin Schwartzrock

405

406

407

408

409

410

411

412

405: COMPANY: Sophia Georgopoulou Design / CLIENT: Marina Frangkeskidou / DESIGNER: Sophia Georgopoulou / ART DIRECTOR: Sophia Georgopoulou
406: COMPANY: Design Center, Inc. / CLIENT: Feed Buy.com / DESIGNER: Sherwin Schwartzrock / ART DIRECTOR: John Reger
407: COMPANY: Matt Lehman Studio / CLIENT: Luxton Records / DESIGNER: / ART DIRECTOR: Nathan Tasker
408: COMPANY: Pollard Design / DESIGNER: Jeff Pollard
409: COMPANY: Schwartzrock Graphic Arts / CLIENT: BI Worldwide / DESIGNER: Sherwin Schwartzrock
410: COMPANY: Schwartzrock Graphic Arts / CLIENT: BI Worldwide / DESIGNER: Sherwin Schwartzrock
411: COMPANY: Schwartzrock Graphic Arts / CLIENT: Worlds of Wow / DESIGNER: Sherwin Schwartzrock
412: COMPANY: Office / CLIENT: Wee Society / DESIGNER: Office / ART DIRECTOR: Jason Schulte

**FIRM:** JEREMY SLAGLE GRAPHIC DESIGN
**DESIGNER / ILLUSTRATOR:** JEREMY SLAGLE
**WRITERS:** CHRISTINE MYERS, VERB GARDEN
**CLIENT:** GÅNOLA

Gånola claims "If we can't spell it, we don't use it," peanut butter, honey, oats, coconut, almonds, whole bran, cranberries, sunflower seeds, blueberries, green tea, coffee beans, bacon, apples, real maple syrup, whole oats, and cinnamon: That's it.

"Our brand name is derived from the Swedish term *gå*, which means 'tread.' Since, as active outdoors people and amateur environmentalists, we firmly believe in utilizing the world as our playground while treading lightly on the Earth and leaving as little footprint as possible."

**gånola**

When it comes to natural or earth-friendly subject matters you normally see design approaches that are more organic. But this is a nice break from that predictable approach. The aesthetic they used is clean, simple, and iconic. This aligns with Gånola's underline choice of ingredients and vision in that respect and reinforces the premise of their name as well.

In an age that is digitally driven, it's nice to see ideas thoroughly explored in analog form. Looking at these thumbnail sketches you can see several directions that could have equally been refined and executed into other nice design solutions on this project as well.

*I think the shelf presence for this POS packaging is sophisticated yet fun. It's not cluttered with trite marketing lingo, or annoying bursts—it lets the branding do the heavy lifting in regards to communication, and the iconography helps to quickly identify the specific flavor being sold.*

*The overall packaging for each individual flavor works well as a brand family while distinctly establishing the individuality of each product member.*

*The established brand colors used on each SKU work well, creating a cohesive product line. Secondary brand elements such as the iconography used to distinguish flavors and ingredients, brings a nice touch of fun to the branding as a whole. Having the actual product showing through the diecut window creates a nice visual contrast with the simplified nature of the packaging.*

413

414

415

416

417

418

419

**UTAP**
PRINTING CO., INC.

420

T E R R A M E S A
R E S O R T   P R O P E R T I E S

421

PROJECT
**HOPE**
WORLDWIDE

422

**munify mobile**

423

424

J .  H I L B U R N
MEN'S CLOTHIER

425

426

**420:** COMPANY: 5Seven / CLIENT: UTAP Printing / DESIGNER: Clint G. Delapaz / ART DIRECTOR: Clint G. Delapaz
**421:** COMPANY: Jon Flaming Design / CLIENT: Terramesa / DESIGNER: Jon Flaming / ART DIRECTOR: Jon Flaming
**422:** COMPANY: Jon Flaming Design / CLIENT: Project Hope / DESIGNER: Jon Flaming / ART DIRECTOR: Jon Flaming
**423:** COMPANY: DesignUnion / CLIENT: Munify Mobile / DESIGNER: Renee Melton
**424:** COMPANY: Jon Flaming Design / CLIENT: Friends of the River / DESIGNER: Jon Flaming / ART DIRECTOR: Jon Flaming
**425:** COMPANY: Jon Flaming Design / CLIENT: J Hilburn / DESIGNER: Jon Flaming / ART DIRECTOR: Jon Flaming
**426:** COMPANY: Jon Flaming Design / CLIENT: Michael Cerny / DESIGNER: Jon Flaming / ART DIRECTOR: Jon Flaming

# Logo Gallery

427

428

429

430

431

432

433

434

**427:** COMPANY: Luke Bott Design & Illustration / CLIENT: Mark Philbrick / DESIGNER: Luke Bott
**428:** COMPANY: Tim Frame Design / CLIENT: Redcast / DESIGNER: Tim Frame / ART DIRECTOR: Tim Frame
**429:** COMPANY: Device / CLIENT: 5 by 5 / DESIGNER: Rian Hughes / ART DIRECTOR: Rian Hughes
**430:** COMPANY: Michael Doret Graphic Design / CLIENT: 1933 Group / DESIGNER: Michael Doret / ART DIRECTOR: Bobby Green
**431:** COMPANY: REACTOR design Studio / CLIENT: Growing Gratitude / DESIGNERS: Chase Wilson, Patrick Drake / ART DIRECTOR: Clifton Alexander
**432:** COMPANY: Invisible Creature / CLIENT: Roadrunner Records / DESIGNER: Ryan Clark / ART DIRECTOR: Ryan Clark
**432:** COMPANY: R&R Partners / CLIENT: R&R Partners / DESIGNER: Randy Heil / ART DIRECTOR: Randy Heil
**434:** COMPANY: Pacey + Pacey Design / CLIENT: North Vancouver Football Club / DESIGNER: Robert Pacey / ART DIRECTOR: Michael Pacey

GLOBAL **BAZAAR** 20 3 07

TREASURES FROM THE ENDS OF THE EARTH

435

436

# CAMP
**Busch Gardens**

437

438

439

440

NOVARTIS
INCENTIVES

441

442

**443**

**444**

**445**

**446**

**447**

**448**

**449**

**443:** COMPANY: J Sayles Design Co. / CLIENT: Roosevelt High School / DESIGNER: John Sayles / ART DIRECTOR: John Sayles
**444:** COMPANY: Design Center, Inc. / CLIENT: Leef / DESIGNER: Sherwin Schwartzrock / ART DIRECTOR: John Reger
**445:** COMPANY: Schwartzrock Graphic Arts / CLIENT: Yanovick, Inc. / DESIGNER: Sherwin Schwartzrock
**446:** COMPANY: Sean Heisler / CLIENT: Sharebaby / DESIGNER: Sean Heisler / ART DIRECTOR: Sean Heisler
**447:** COMPANY: Schwartzrock Graphic Arts / CLIENT: Nobel Communications / DESIGNER: Sherwin Schwartzrock
**448:** COMPANY: Schwartzrock Graphic Arts / CLIENT: Nazarene Publishing House / DESIGNER: Sherwin Schwartzrock
**449:** COMPANY: Schwartzrock Graphic Arts / CLIENT: Home Brewed Candle Co. / DESIGNER: Sherwin Schwartzrock

450

ROCKET
GOLF

451

452

453

WESTWOOD

454

455

450: COMPANY: Sean Heisler / CLIENT: iPracticeMD / DESIGNER: Sean Heisler / ART DIRECTOR: Sean Heisler
451: COMPANY: Salvadore Anguiano / CLIENT: Kaiko Furniture Design / DESIGNER: Salvadore Anguiano / ART DIRECTOR: Salvadore Anguiano
452: COMPANY: Schwartzrock Graphic Arts / CLIENT: Windworks, Inc. / DESIGNER: Sherwin Schwartzrock
453: COMPANY: Sean Heisler / CLIENT: Katapult Design / DESIGNER: Sean Heisler / ART DIRECTOR: Sean Heisler
454: COMPANY: Schwartzrock Graphic Arts / CLIENT: Westwood Lutheran Church / DESIGNER: Sherwin Schwartzrock
455: COMPANY: Schwartzrock Graphic Arts / CLIENT: Mike Mahoney / DESIGNER: Sherwin Schwartzrock

WIESE

COMMUNICATIONS

456

ZION
GROVE
23988 ZION AVENUE

457

THE WRAP UP
2008

458

ESTD 1978

LEADERSHIP
FOUNDATIONS

459

RUSSELL
SIMPSON
INC

460

EXPLORERS
CHRISTOPHER COLUMBUS CHARTER SCHOOL

461

SUPER
SOLUTIONS

462

BURNING
BRIDGE
TAVERN
WRIGHTSVILLE • PENNSYLVANIA

463

**456:** COMPANY: Schwartzrock Graphic Arts / CLIENT: Wiese Creative / DESIGNER: Sherwin Schwartzrock
**457:** COMPANY: Schwartzrock Graphic Arts / CLIENT: Dr. Jim and Mary Neff / DESIGNER: Sherwin Schwartzrock
**458:** COMPANY: Schwartzrock Graphic Arts / CLIENT: BI Worldwide / DESIGNER: Sherwin Schwartzrock
**459:** COMPANY: Sussner Design Company / CLIENT: Leadership Foundations / DESIGNER: Brandon Van Lieve / ART DIRECTOR: Derek Sussner
**460:** COMPANY: Wonderwheel Creative / CLIENT: Russell Simpson, Inc. / DESIGNER: Sarah Lotus Trainor / ART DIRECTOR: Tim Merrill
**461:** COMPANY: Scott Oeschger / CLIENT: Christopher Columbus Charter School / DESIGNER: Scott Oeschger / ART DIRECTOR: Scott Oeschger
**462:** COMPANY: Design Center, Inc. / CLIENT: Super Solutions / DESIGNER: Sherwin Schwartzrock / ART DIRECTOR: John Reger
**463:** COMPANY: Sparkfly Creative / CLIENT: Burning Bridge Tavern / DESIGNER: John Ferguson / ART DIRECTOR: John Ferguson

464

465

466

467

468

469

470

471

**464:** COMPANY: Schwartzrock Graphic Arts / CLIENT: Deep Down, Inc. / DESIGNER: Sherwin Schwartzrock
**465:** COMPANY: Schwartzrock Graphic Arts / CLIENT: BI Worldwide / DESIGNER: Sherwin Schwartzrock
**466:** COMPANY: Schwartzrock Graphic Arts / CLIENT: BI Worldwide / DESIGNER: Sherwin Schwartzrock
**467:** COMPANY: Schwartzrock Graphic Arts / CLIENT: RiverBrand Design / DESIGNER: Sherwin Schwartzrock
**468:** COMPANY: Schwartzrock Graphic Arts / CLIENT: American Bible Society / DESIGNER: Sherwin Schwartzrock
**469:** COMPANY: Logo Turn / DESIGNER: Gregory Grigoriou / ART DIRECTOR: Gregory Grigoriou
**470:** COMPANY: Design Center, Inc. / CLIENT: Shada Arabian Sanction / DESIGNER: Sherwin Schwartzrock / ART DIRECTOR: John Reger
**471:** COMPANY: Schwartzrock Graphic Arts / CLIENT: OLSON Denali Advertising / DESIGNER: Sherwin Schwartzrock / ART DIRECTOR:

**FIRM:** JOE BOSACK GRAPHIC DESIGN
**DESIGNER / ILLUSTRATOR:** JOE BOSACK
**CLIENT:** UW STEVEN'S POINT

UW–Steven's Point is one of thirteen campuses in the University of Wisconsin system. With new leadership in place and a renewed focus on athletics, UWSP sought a new identity that would have them stand out from the crowded Wisconsin collegiate landscape.

Already enriched with a unique nickname, Pointers, we set out to create an equally unique identity to represent it. Early research and discovery uncovered a highly competitive athletic program represented by dozens of different logos created over the course of many years. The result was an incoherent identity that had each sport looking different from the rest.

Our initial exploration included numerous perspectives and poses with the final identity being a strong, bold, and simple profile of the pointer. The primary logo is accompanied by a system of closely related secondary and word logos that allows the identity to function cohesively across a wide range of applications.

UW-STEVENS POINT
POINTERS

*Bold, strong, and straightforward is captured well in this sports identity. Bosack pulls off a unique utilitarian motif that represents the school well and establishes a strong mascot the school can market itself with for years to come.*

*This mark could have taken many directions and there are several solid designs being explored in this early stage of the creative process.*

The brand system is perfectly suited for the school's many sports programs and this shows how this type of usage would work on both a colored and white background. The design has a nice capacity to simplify into a one-color mark and still carry the full weight of the new branding. That is easier said than done, and this does it well.

Further design directions and color applications round out the final presentation of potential brand graphics presented to UWSP.

The ease of use is clearly seen in this mark's usage across a broad range of applications such as apparel, and interior locations such as the gym floor.

## The HONORS GOLF CLUB
### DALLAS, TEXAS

472

473

SEECREATURE

475

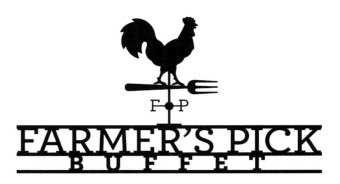

## FARMER'S PICK BUFFET

474

type **A**

476

477

## VERITEX BANK

478

**472:** COMPANY: Jon Flaming Design / CLIENT: Urbana / DESIGNER: Jon Flaming / ART DIRECTOR: Jon Flaming
**473:** COMPANY: The Joe Bosack Graphic Design Co. / DESIGNER: Joe Bosack / ART DIRECTOR: Joe Bosack
**474:** COMPANY: M&M / CLIENT: Isle of Capri Casinos, Inc. / DESIGNER: Scott Oeschger / ART DIRECTOR: Scott Oeschger
**475:** COMPANY: Jon Flaming Design / CLIENT: SeaCreature / DESIGNER: Jon Flaming / ART DIRECTOR: Jon Flaming
**476:** CLIENT: Type A / DESIGNER: Chris Rooney
**477:** COMPANY: The Joe Bosack Graphic Design Co. / DESIGNER: Joe Bosack / ART DIRECTOR: Joe Bosack
**478:** COMPANY: Jon Flaming Design / CLIENT: Veritex / DESIGNER: Jon Flaming / ART DIRECTOR: Jon Flaming

479

yellow**robin**
M A R K E T I N G

480

481

M
metro

482

performance **labs**

483

FLORIDA REALTORS

484

CAMP FIRE

485

479: COMPANY: Kris Bazen Creative / CLIENT: The Samurai Conquistadors / DESIGNER: Kris Bazen / ART DIRECTOR: Kris Bazen
480: COMPANY: Duct Tape & Glitter / CLIENT: Yellow Robin / DESIGNER: Luke Bott
481: COMPANY: Storefront Political Media / CLIENT: Reset SF / DESIGNER: Clint G. Delapaz / ART DIRECTOR: Clint G. Delapaz
482: COMPANY: M3AD.com / CLIENT: Chronos / DESIGNER: Dan McElhattan III / ART DIRECTOR: Dan McElhattan III
483: COMPANY: AuhDesign / CLIENT: Mezzo Labs / DESIGNER: Hyun Auh / ART DIRECTOR: Hyun Auh
484: COMPANY: Jon Flaming Design / CLIENT: Florida Realtors / DESIGNER: Jon Flaming / ART DIRECTOR: Jon Flaming
485: COMPANY: Jon Flaming Design / CLIENT: Campfire / DESIGNER: Jon Flaming / ART DIRECTOR: Jon Flaming

MEASUREMENT AND CONTROL

486

487

488

489

INSOMNIA
entertainment

490

491

492

493

**486:** COMPANY: REACTOR design Studio / CLIENT: SOR / DESIGNER: Chase Wilson / ART DIRECTOR: Clifton Alexander
**487:** COMPANY: Device / CLIENT: Mercury Records / DESIGNER: Rian Hughes / ART DIRECTOR: Rian Hughes
**488:** COMPANY: Donatelli / CLIENT: Temdel Typographics / DESIGNER: Steve Donatelli / ART DIRECTOR: Steve Donatelli
**489:** COMPANY: Sean Heisler / CLIENT: Sideburn / DESIGNER: Sean Heisler / ART DIRECTOR: Sean Heisler
**490:** COMPANY: Schwartzrock Graphic Arts / CLIENT: BI Worldwide / DESIGNER: Sherwin Schwartzrock
**491:** COMPANY: R&R Partners / CLIENT: Insomnia Entertainment / DESIGNER: Randy Heil / ART DIRECTOR: Randy Heil
**492:** COMPANY: Invisible Creature / CLIENT: Invisible Creature / DESIGNER: Ryan Clark / ART DIRECTOR: Ryan Clark
**493:** COMPANY: R&R Partners / CLIENT: Jitters Gourmet Coffee / DESIGNER: Randy Heil / ART DIRECTOR: Randy Heil

494

495

496

497

498

499

500

501

**494:** COMPANY: Rule29 / CLIENT: DNA Astronaut / DESIGNER: Tim Damitz / ART DIRECTOR: Justin Ahrens
**495:** COMPANY: Pacey + Pacey Design / CLIENT: UBC Library Vault / DESIGNER: Robert Pacey / ART DIRECTOR: Michael Pacey
**496:** COMPANY: / CLIENT: Penfield / DESIGNER: Bryan Danknich / ART DIRECTOR: Mike Calkins
**497:** COMPANY: Design Center, Inc. / DESIGNER: Sherwin Schwartzrock / ART DIRECTOR: John Reger
**498:** COMPANY: BrandLtd.com / CLIENT: Shinasha / DESIGNER: Jordan Kobalka / ART DIRECTOR: Paul Rippens
**499:** COMPANY: Mint / CLIENT: Target / DESIGNER: Mike Calkins
**500:** COMPANY: R&R Partners / CLIENT: Busch Entertainment Corp. / DESIGNER: Randy Heil / ART DIRECTOR: Randy Heil
**501:** COMPANY: Invisible Creature / CLIENT: Sasquatch! Music Festival / DESIGNER: Don Clark / ART DIRECTOR: Don Clark

ISAIAH 40:31

**CCS**

COMMUNITY
CHRISTIAN
SCHOOL

502

Town

503

STUDENT SUSTAINED ✶ URBAN AGRICULTURE

**THE FARM PROJECT**

GROWING OUR OWN

504

C I T Y L I F E

505

THE **KINGDOM** SAGA

506

MAROON5

507

SOUTHERN ✶ OILFIELD
**COOKERS**

DEEP DOWN
INC.

508

**502:** COMPANY: Schwartzrock Graphic Arts / CLIENT: Community Christian School / DESIGNER: Sherwin Schwartzrock
**503:** COMPANY: Thrillustrate
**504:** COMPANY: Timber Design Co. / DESIGNER: Lars Lawson
**505:** COMPANY: Six.22 / CLIENT: Citylife Ministries / DESIGNER: Jamie Vetter / ART DIRECTOR: Jamie Vetter
**506:** COMPANY: Schwartzrock Graphic Arts / CLIENT: American Bible Society / DESIGNER: Sherwin Schwartzrock
**507:** COMPANY: Mattson Creative / DESIGNER: Ty Mattson
**508:** COMPANY: Schwartzrock Graphic Arts / CLIENT: Deep Down, Inc. / DESIGNER: Sherwin Schwartzrock

509

510

JEREMY CHARLES

511

512

LOVE'S GARDEN

513

514

509: COMPANY: Weather Control / CLIENT: Touloukion Guitars / DESIGNER: Josh Oakley
510: COMPANY: Schwartzrock Graphic Arts / CLIENT: BI Worldwide / DESIGNER: Sherwin Schwartzrock
511: COMPANY: TY Design / CLIENT: Jeremy Charles Photography / DESIGNER: Ty Wilkins / ART DIRECTOR: Ty Wilkins
512: COMPANY: Schwartzrock Graphic Arts / CLIENT: Design Center / DESIGNER: Sherwin Schwartzrock
513: COMPANY: Schwartzrock Graphic Arts / CLIENT: Love's Garden / DESIGNER: Sherwin Schwartzrock
514: COMPANY: Design Center, Inc. / CLIENT: Cameleon / DESIGNER: Sherwin Schwartzrock / ART DIRECTOR: John Reger

515

516

517

518

519

520

521

522

523

524

HAND AND FOOT CARE

525

526

527

528

529

530

523: COMPANY: Schwartzrock Graphic Arts / CLIENT: MN Health and Housing Association / DESIGNER: Sherwin Schwartzrock
524: COMPANY: Schwartzrock Graphic Arts / CLIENT: Nobel Communications / DESIGNER: Sherwin Schwartzrock
525: COMPANY: Sophia Georgopoulou Design / CLIENT: waterlily spa / DESIGNER: Sophia Georgopoulou / ART DIRECTOR: Sophia Georgopoulou
526: CLIENT: Rio Products / DESIGNER: Jacob Carter / ART DIRECTOR: Mike Calkins
527: COMPANY: Schwartzrock Graphic Arts / CLIENT: Initio3i / DESIGNER: Sherwin Schwartzrock
528: COMPANY: Schwartzrock Graphic Arts / CLIENT: Kingstone Media / DESIGNER: Sherwin Schwartzrock
529: COMPANY: Schwartzrock Graphic Arts / CLIENT: Design Center / DESIGNER: Sherwin Schwartzrock
530: COMPANY: Design Center, Inc. / CLIENT: Bailey Nurseries / DESIGNER: Sherwin Schwartzrock / ART DIRECTOR: John Reger

**FIRM:** JON FLAMING DESIGN
**DESIGNER / ILLUSTRATOR:** JON FLAMING
**CLIENT:** ARRINGTON OUTDOOR

Our assignment was to create a memorable logo for Arrington Outdoor Advertising that would be bold graphically and would also convey a feeling of stability and strength. Arrington Outdoor Advertising is an independent billboard company with strategic billboard locations along major freeways and rural highways all over Texas.

Within only a few years of launching their new brand, Arrington Outdoor has become one of the fastest growing outdoor board companies in Texas. Their billboards provide bold and powerful images that cannot be turned off and are always on your mind.

*These sketches with hints of retro visual cues would have given Arrington an immediate sense that the company has a rich corporate heritage.*

These two sketches are smart options to show. The first feels very whimsical in style, but perfectly demonstrates in one "lock up" what it is that Arrington accomplishes.

The second conveys stability and strength, as the brief demanded. The overtly bold Atlaslike figure holding up a billboard instantly relates the company's message. The rendering style here would play a big role in showing its audience a good balance between the company's competitiveness and playfulness.

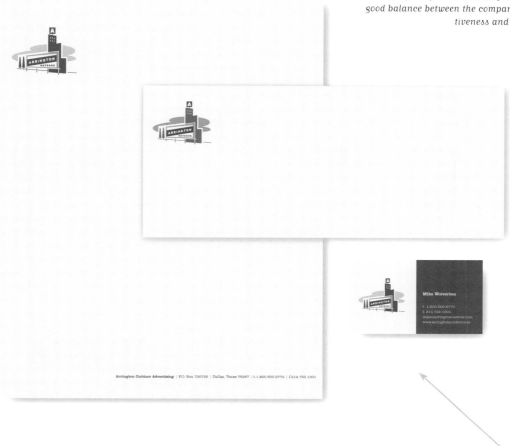

The final mark is a perfect blend of nostalgia-meets-sophistication. With a logo that leans illustrative, you don't want to go over the top with the stationery application graphics. The sparse type treatment, the airy breakup of the space, and subdued color palette finish this identity off with a genius level exercise of restraint.

# Logo Gallery

531

532

533

534

535

536

537

538

539

540

Risk

541

542

543

544

**538:** COMPANY: Adam Anderson / DESIGNER: Adam Anderson
**539:** COMPANY: The Joe Bosack Graphic Design Co. / DESIGNER: Joe Bosack / ART DIRECTOR: Joe Bosack
**540:** COMPANY: Invisible Creature / CLIENT: Foo Fighters / DESIGNER: Don Clark / ART DIRECTOR: Don Clark
**541:** COMPANY: Mint / CLIENT: Risk / DESIGNER: Mike Calkins
**542:** COMPANY: Jon Flaming Design / CLIENT: David Arrington / DESIGNER: Jon Flaming / ART DIRECTOR: Jon Flaming
**543:** COMPANY: Allis Collective / CLIENT: Raymond Renaissance / DESIGNER: Clint G. Delapaz / ART DIRECTOR: Remy Allis
**544:** COMPANY: Pollard Design / DESIGNER: Jeff Pollard

545

WONDERKIND

S T U D I O S

546

547

548

549

550

551

552

545: COMPANY: Fernandez Studio / CLIENT: Lincoln Park Zoo / DESIGNER: Carlos Fernandez / ART DIRECTOR: Peggy Martin
546: COMPANY: Rule29 / CLIENT: WonderKind Studios / DESIGNER: Kara Ayarum / ART DIRECTOR: Justin Ahrens
547: COMPANY: Thrillustrate / CLIENT: Homeless Ministry
548: COMPANY: Jeremy Slagle Graphic Design / CLIENT: Columbus Cutters Scooter Club / DESIGNER: Jeremy Slagle / ART DIRECTOR: Jeremy Slagle
549: COMPANY: Throttle Design Mechanics / CLIENT: Scat Enterprises / DESIGNERS: John Nissen, Dave Adamson / ART DIRECTOR: Dave Adamson
550: COMPANY: Tim Frame Design / CLIENT: Roger Schultz / DESIGNER: Tim Frame / ART DIRECTOR: Roger Schultz
551: COMPANY: R&R Partners / CLIENT: Pete Ernaut / DESIGNER: Randy Heil / ART DIRECTOR: Randy Heil
552: COMPANY: Mint / CLIENT: Penfield / DESIGNER: Bryan Danknich

553

554

555

556

557

558

559

560

553: COMPANY: Tim Frame Design / CLIENT: Schottenstein Property Group / DESIGNER: Tim Frame / ART DIRECTOR: Rebecca Reeder
554: CLIENT: Tatyana Baidak / DESIGNER: Artem Dvorzhak
555: COMPANY: Salvadore Anguiano / CLIENT: Bô Salon / DESIGNER: Salvadore Anguiano / ART DIRECTOR: Salvadore Anguiano
556: COMPANY: Device / CLIENT: DC Comics / DESIGNER: Rian Hughes / ART DIRECTOR: Mark Chiarello
557: COMPANY: Varsity Mascot Company / CLIENT: Chavez Elementary School / DESIGNERS: Sam Sedor, Ryan Welty / ART DIRECTOR: Dave Adamson
558: COMPANY: Device / CLIENT: Yvonne Neuman / DESIGNER: Rian Hughes / ART DIRECTOR: Rian Hughes
559: COMPANY: Mint / CLIENT: Benni's / DESIGNER: Bryan Danknich / ART DIRECTOR: Mike Calkins
560: COMPANY: Varsity Mascot Company / CLIENT: Jefferson High School / DESIGNERS: Wendel Hayes, Ryan Welty / ART DIRECTOR: Dave Adamson

561

562

563

564

565

566

567

**561:** COMPANY: Schwartzrock Graphic Arts / CLIENT: Freshwater Church / DESIGNER: Sherwin Schwartzrock
**562:** COMPANY: Schwartzrock Graphic Arts / CLIENT: Werner Design Werks / DESIGNER: Sherwin Schwartzrock
**563:** COMPANY: R&R Partners / CLIENT: Las Vegas Arts District / DESIGNER: Randy Heil / ART DIRECTOR: Randy Heil
**564:** COMPANY: Adam Anderson / DESIGNER: Adam Anderson
**565:** COMPANY: Schwartzrock Graphic Arts / CLIENT: Tim Westermeyer / DESIGNER: Sherwin Schwartzrock
**566:** COMPANY: Schwartzrock Graphic Arts / CLIENT: Bing Puddlepot / DESIGNER: Sherwin Schwartzrock
**567:** COMPANY: Schwartzrock Graphic Arts / CLIENT: BI Worldwide / DESIGNER: Sherwin Schwartzrock

Energy

 Transportation

 Real Estate

 Agriculture

 Land

 Water

568

LUTHERAN GLOBAL MEDIA

569

ENHANCED
LANDSCAPING

571

570

**Enhanced**
LANDSCAPING

572

573

**568:** COMPANY: Gee + Chung Design / CLIENT: Equilibrium Capital / DESIGNER: Earl Gee / ART DIRECTOR: Earl Gee
**569:** COMPANY: Schwartzrock Graphic Arts / CLIENT: Lutheran Global Media / DESIGNER: Sherwin Schwartzrock
**570:** COMPANY: Schwartzrock Graphic Arts / CLIENT: 81 Worldwide / DESIGNER: Sherwin Schwartzrock
**571:** COMPANY: Schwartzrock Graphic Arts / CLIENT: Enhanced Landscaping / DESIGNER: Sherwin Schwartzrock
**572:** COMPANY: Schwartzrock Graphic Arts / CLIENT: Enhanced Landscaping / DESIGNER: Sherwin Schwartzrock
**573:** COMPANY: Schwartzrock Graphic Arts / CLIENT: Community Comics / DESIGNER: Sherwin Schwartzrock

574

575

576

577

578

579

580

581

**574:** COMPANY: Schwartzrock Graphic Arts / CLIENT: Vibrant Cycles / DESIGNER: Sherwin Schwartzrock
**575:** COMPANY: Schwartzrock Graphic Arts / CLIENT: Design Center / DESIGNER: Sherwin Schwartzrock
**576:** COMPANY: Schwartzrock Graphic Arts / CLIENT: RiverBrand Design / DESIGNER: Sherwin Schwartzrock
**577:** COMPANY: Schwartzrock Graphic Arts / CLIENT: RiverBrand Design / DESIGNER: Sherwin Schwartzrock
**578:** COMPANY: Schwartzrock Graphic Arts / CLIENT: Yanovick, Inc. / DESIGNER: Sherwin Schwartzrock /
**579:** COMPANY: Schwartzrock Graphic Arts / CLIENT: Freshwater Church / DESIGNER: Sherwin Schwartzrock
**580:** COMPANY: Design Center, Inc. / CLIENT: Shada Arabian Sanction / DESIGNER: Sherwin Schwartzrock / ART DIRECTOR: John Reger
**581:** COMPANY: Design Center, Inc. / CLIENT: St. Croix Sensory / DESIGNER: Sherwin Schwartzrock / ART DIRECTOR: John Reger

582

583

THE FRONT ROOM
A PARK CITIES DINER

584

585

586

587

SCENE ON MAIN
URBAN. COCKTAILS. CUISINE.

588

589

582: COMPANY: Schwartzrock Graphic Arts / CLIENT: Initio Advertising / DESIGNER: Sherwin Schwartzrock
583: COMPANY: Schwartzrock Graphic Arts / CLIENT: Pugleasa Company / DESIGNER: Sherwin Schwartzrock
584: COMPANY: Banowetz & Company / CLIENT: The Front Room / DESIGNER: Eric Venegas / ART DIRECTOR: Eric Venegas
585: COMPANY: Schwartzrock Graphic Arts / CLIENT: Wiese Communications / DESIGNER: Sherwin Schwartzrock
586: COMPANY: Schwartzrock Graphic Arts / CLIENT: BI Worldwide / DESIGNER: Sherwin Schwartzrock
587: COMPANY: Schwartzrock Graphic Arts / CLIENT: BI Worldwide / DESIGNER: Sherwin Schwartzrock
588: COMPANY: Banowetz & Company / CLIENT: Scene on Main / DESIGNER: Eric Venegas / ART DIRECTOR: Eric Venegas
589: COMPANY: Helveticka / CLIENT: Visiontec / DESIGNER: Sherwin Schwartzrock / ART DIRECTOR: John Mraz

# Designer Blind Spots

BILL GARDNER

a

b

c

d

For more than a decade now I have written the LogoLounge Logo Trend Report, published annually to our site and to hundreds of journals and websites around the world. As anticipated as it is, there is always a fringe element that responds with a missive that if it's a trend, any designer worth their salt should disregard it. Their premise is generally that great design ignores the currents and sets a course diametric to the flow. Usually these same comments come from the designers that profess superior design is a result of batter mixed in a vacuum.

These reports are created to give logo designers a snapshot of where they are in time. Every report starts with a qualifier, "These trends are not reported to be imitated." They are created so a cogent follower of the craft is able to move a line of thought forward—so they can make a design decision that is informed and will meet with success.

Ask a studied member of the identity fraternity about the history of a mark and they will be able to track the seminal influences backward like a bloodhound. They can tell you what begat what and who begat who because they lived through the changes and were themselves affected in their own design. Why did logos in the late '80s have speed lines running through them (fig a)? Why was most early '90s design replete with ziggurats and pulpy paper? How did the Lucent Technologies circle (fig b), BP flower (fig c), and the MSN butterfly logo (fig d) shift our perspective of design in the beginning of this century? Even better, what does it matter? It matters.

Like a Monday morning quarterback, it's much easier to relay history than to predict the future. In a backward view we seldom are surprised by factors of influence or their impact. All the points of contact and inner connecting cogwheels make perfect sense when there is context. But why can't we see it coming? Did those designers who did design the logo that changed the landscape know what they were doing? Did they just get lucky or was it a bit of both?

There's an old line that says "It's better to be lucky than it is to be smart." I think identity designers that consistently produce effective forward thinking design do it because they have a different way of reacting to the environment. They are not looking at what's being done to see how they can apply it. They are looking at what is being done to see how they can move it forward. And this is where the secret comes in. Whether intuitive or calculated, they look at how a current trend came to be and determine where it is going, based on trajectory.

If you see a specific trend that has been emerging over a period of time and you identify a progression in its change, then you can extrapolate where that progression is headed. I liken this to someone being shown a map with a dot on a road representing a car on a trip. Ask them to speculate where the driver is headed. It's little more than a crap shoot. Then show the same person where the car was the previous day and suddenly you know which direction they are headed, and their speed and the challenge is much easier. Guessing the trajectory of an object in motion from a single snapshot is impossible.

Plot where a design trend comes from and how it evolved to where it is now. It's much more likely you'll predict a path to show you where it will be in the future. These designers don't keep a folder of charts to accomplish this. They are just tuned into design in such a way as to best utilize this past knowledge as they are looking for what's next.

This is why I report logo trends. Follow the trajectories of an idea to the next destination. It might take you somewhere you don't agree with or to a place the world is not yet prepared to visit. But the designer that uses yesterday's answers for today's problems won't be designing for tomorrow's audience.

590

HULU

591

592

593

LACERTUS
CAFE·BISTRO

594

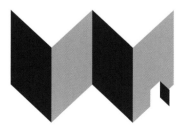

595

596

590: COMPANY: Greteman Group / CLIENT: Lewis Energy Group / DESIGNER: Garrett Fresh / ART DIRECTOR: Sonia Greteman
591: COMPANY: Owen Jones Design / CLIENT: Hulu / DESIGNER: Owen Jones / ART DIRECTOR: Owen Jones
592: COMPANY: Tim Frame Design / CLIENT: Heroes of the Nation / DESIGNER: Tim Frame / ART DIRECTOR: Tim Frame
593: COMPANY: Jon Flaming Design / CLIENT: Slingshot / DESIGNER: Jon Flaming / ART DIRECTOR: Jon Flaming
594: COMPANY: Chris Trivizas / CLIENT: Yannis Zerbas / DESIGNER: Chris Trivizas / ART DIRECTOR: Chris Trivizas
595: COMPANY: Green Ideals / CLIENT: Wiegel Law Group / DESIGNER: Clint G. Delapaz / ART DIRECTOR: Susan Bierzychudek
596: COMPANY: Art Chantry Design / CLIENT: Stussy / DESIGNER: Art Chantry / ART DIRECTOR: Art Chantry

597

598

599

600

# NACHT & LEWIS

601

602

603

597: COMPANY: Casualty / CLIENT: Redeeming Soles / DESIGNER: Steve Gaines
598: COMPANY: Jon Flaming Design / CLIENT: Urbana / DESIGNER: Jon Flaming / ART DIRECTOR: Jon Flaming
599: COMPANY: chameleon design / CLIENT: Nancy Bridged / DESIGNER: Tomas Vateha / ART DIRECTOR: Tomas Vateha
600: COMPANY: AkinsTudio / CLIENT: City of Norcross, Georgia / DESIGNER: Charles Akins / ART DIRECTOR: Charles Akins
601: COMPANY: Mode Design / CLIENT: Nacht & Lewis / DESIGNER: Hans Bennewitz, Steven Fong / ART DIRECTOR: Hans Bennewitz
602: COMPANY: The Joe Bosack Graphic Design Co. / DESIGNER: Joe Bosack / ART DIRECTOR: Joe Bosack
603: COMPANY: Jon Flaming Design / CLIENT: Urbana Communities / DESIGNER: Jon Flaming / ART DIRECTOR: Jon Flaming

604

MIAMI VALLEY HOSPITAL

BABY OLYMPICS

605

606

## ARCHER
### HOME INSPECTION
& ENVIRONMENTAL SERVICES

607

608

609

610

611

612

613

614

615

616

617

618

619

**612:** COMPANY: J Sayles Design Co. / CLIENT: Bone-A-Patreat / DESIGNER: John Sayles / ART DIRECTOR: John Sayles
**613:** COMPANY: Michael Doret Graphic Design / CLIENT: Graphic Artists Guild / DESIGNER: Michael Doret / ART DIRECTOR: Simms Taback
**614:** COMPANY: Base Art Co. / CLIENT: Resource Interactive / DESIGNER: Terry Rohrback / ART DIRECTOR: Terry Rohrback
**615:** CLIENT: Tacorama / DESIGNER: Artem Dvorzhak / ART DIRECTOR:
**616:** COMPANY: Timber Design Co. / DESIGNER: Lars Lawson / ART DIRECTOR:
**617:** COMPANY: Baji Group / CLIENT: Redemption Church / DESIGNER: Jonny Ashcroft
**618:** CLIENT: Dankins Ice Cream / DESIGNER: Mike Calkins
**619:** CLIENT: Target Stores - Bunny / DESIGNER: Jacob Carter / ART DIRECTOR: Mike Calkins

**CAMP**

SEAWORLD ★ BUSCH GARDENS

620

621

622

623

624

625

626

**620:** COMPANY: R&R Partners / CLIENT: Busch Entertainment Corp. / DESIGNER: Randy Heil / ART DIRECTOR: Randy Heil
**621:** COMPANY: Mint / CLIENT: Hilliards Brewery / DESIGNER: Bryan Danknich / ART DIRECTOR: Mike Calkins
**622:** COMPANY: Schwartzrock Graphic Arts / CLIENT: Design Center / DESIGNER: Sherwin Schwartzrock
**623:** COMPANY: Mint / CLIENT: Main Dish / DESIGNER: Mike Calkins
**624:** COMPANY: leightonhubbell.com / CLIENT: Motive Group / DESIGNER: Leighton Hubbell / ART DIRECTOR: Leighton Hubbell
**625:** COMPANY: R&R Partners / CLIENT: Springs Preserve / DESIGNER: Randy Heil / ART DIRECTOR: Randy Heil
**626:** COMPANY: Schwartzrock Graphic Arts / CLIENT: IPG / DESIGNER: Sherwin Schwortzrock

627

**Tampa Bay**

628

**RED HEN** TRAVEL

629

630

**MR. MULLET**

631

BRAD **RADIKE**

632

**627:** COMPANY: leightonhubbell.com / CLIENT: Nectar Labs / DESIGNER: Leighton Hubbell / ART DIRECTOR: Leighton Hubbell
**628:** COMPANY: R&R Partners / CLIENT: Tampa Bay Tourism / DESIGNER: Randy Heil / ART DIRECTOR: Randy Heil
**629:** COMPANY: Design Center, Inc. / CLIENT: Design Center / DESIGNER: Sherwin Schwartzrock / ART DIRECTOR: John Reger
**630:** COMPANY: Flight Deck Creative / CLIENT: T Awards / DESIGNER: Jason Rahn / ART DIRECTOR: Jason Rahn
**631:** COMPANY: R&R Partners / CLIENT: Pat Carrigan / DESIGNER: Randy Heil / ART DIRECTOR: Randy Heil
**632:** COMPANY: Schwartzrock Graphic Arts / CLIENT: Brad Radtke / DESIGNER: Sherwin Schwartzrock

633

634

635

636

637

638

639

640

**633:** COMPANY: Schwartzrock Graphic Arts / CLIENT: BI Worldwide / DESIGNER: Sherwin Schwartzrock
**634:** COMPANY: Schwartzrock Graphic Arts / CLIENT: BI Worldwide / DESIGNER: Sherwin Schwartzrock
**635:** COMPANY: Charpentier Hovland Advertising / CLIENT: Fever Basketball / DESIGNER: Sherwin Schwartzrock / ART DIRECTOR: Shannon Charpentier
**636:** COMPANY: Schwartzrock Graphic Arts / CLIENT: BI Worldwide / DESIGNER: Sherwin Schwartzrock
**637:** COMPANY: Design Center, Inc. / CLIENT: Wellspring / DESIGNER: Sherwin Schwartzrock / ART DIRECTOR: John Reger
**638:** COMPANY: Schwartzrock Graphic Arts / CLIENT: Design Center / DESIGNER: Sherwin Schwartzrock
**639:** COMPANY: Schwartzrock Graphic Arts / CLIENT: Hawley High School / DESIGNER: Sherwin Schwartzrock
**640:** COMPANY: Design Center, Inc. / CLIENT: Byerly's and Lunds / DESIGNER: Sherwin Schwartzrock / ART DIRECTOR: John Reger

641

642

643

644

645

646

647

648

**641:** COMPANY: Schwartzrock Graphic Arts / CLIENT: BI Worldwide / DESIGNER: Sherwin Schwartzrock
**642:** COMPANY: Schwartzrock Graphic Arts / CLIENT: Initio Advertising / DESIGNER: Sherwin Schwartzrock
**643:** COMPANY: Schwartzrock Graphic Arts / CLIENT: Dennis Magner / DESIGNER: Sherwin Schwartzrock
**644:** COMPANY: Schwartzrock Graphic Arts / CLIENT: Delphax Technologies / DESIGNER: Sherwin Schwartzrock
**645:** COMPANY: R&R Partners / CLIENT: Busch Entertainment Corp. / DESIGNER: Randy Heil / ART DIRECTOR: Randy Heil
**647:** COMPANY: Schwartzrock Graphic Arts / CLIENT: Vocabra / DESIGNER: Sherwin Schwartzrock
**648:** CLIENT: Visualogistix / DESIGNER: Paul Howalt

**FIRM:** JOSEPH BLALOCK DESIGN
**DESIGNERS:** JOSEPH BLALOCK
**CLIENT:** EXTREMEMUSIC.COM

Hype Production Music is a platform that helps promote relatively unknown musicians to a wider audience of younger fans. The goal of this project was to appeal to this younger fan base by leaning into metaphors and executions that are vibrant and fresh, conceptually relating back to the music itself and lifestyle of the market. Successful logo options needed to work hard at varying sizes, ranging from physical banners down to a small web favicon.

The approach I took at first was to cast the net wide in looking for visual metaphors, not limit my thinking based on end-use sizing. These metaphors ranged in ideas that represented loudness, communication, energy, the lifting of a career, to basic things such as music itself. I looked for a range of bold and vibrant colors that appealed to a younger market, along with subtle gritty textures that contrasted my geometric style. Ultimately, the more successful options worked well in all size requirements, gave a sense of this vibrant and varied music lifestyle, and had conceptual and graphical flexibility to work in varying lockups and positions.

*Hype goes out of its way to purposely snub its graphic nose at identity norms. Funky typography nested in a flame motif and overprinted on spartan san serif type, it's a contrast of the music it represents produced by careless youth with a disregard of established norms.*

*The logo works well in a more simplified format even reducing down to a nice one-color treatment used with an iconic rocket to reinforce the flame concept.*

*Hype cannot be contained within one context of style so Blalock lets it run free and allows the brand to become what it needs to be, more hype playing off visual metaphors and color palettes that expand the brand vernacular.*

649

650

651

652

653

654

655

**649:** COMPANY: Gardner Design / CLIENT: Bluebird Books / DESIGNER: Brian Miller / ART DIRECTOR: Brian Miller
**650:** COMPANY: DesignUnion / CLIENT: Pangea Studios / DESIGNER: Renee Melton
**651:** COMPANY: leightonhubbell.com / CLIENT: Signature Properties / DESIGNER: Leighton Hubbell / ART DIRECTOR: Leighton Hubbell
**652:** COMPANY: chameleon design / CLIENT: Bern Agafi / hairdresser / DESIGNER: Tomáš Vateha / ART DIRECTOR: Tomáš Vateha
**653:** COMPANY: leightonhubbell.com / CLIENT: Spazazz / DESIGNER: Leighton Hubbell / ART DIRECTOR: Leighton Hubbell
**654:** COMPANY: Jon Flaming Design / CLIENT: Watermark Community Church / DESIGNER: Jon Flaming / ART DIRECTOR: Jon Flaming
**655:** COMPANY: The Joe Bosack Graphic Design Co. / CLIENT: / DESIGNER: Joe Bosack / ART DIRECTOR: Joe Bosack

656

657

658

659

CREATE

INNOVATE

INCUBATE

CULTIVATE

EDUCATE

COLLABORATE

660

urbanarte

661

662

656: COMPANY: Tacoma Arts Administration / CLIENT: Amy McBride, City of Tacoma / DESIGNER: Art Chantry / ART DIRECTOR: Art Chantry
657: COMPANY: Chase Design Group / CLIENT: Appinionator / DESIGNER: Margo Chase / ART DIRECTOR: Margo Chase
658: COMPANY: Allis Collective / CLIENT: Raymond Renaissance / DESIGNER: Clint G. Delapaz / ART DIRECTOR: Remy Allis
659: COMPANY: The Joe Bosack Graphic Design Co. / DESIGNER: Joe Bosack / ART DIRECTOR: Joe Bosack
660: COMPANY: Gee + Chung Design / CLIENT: Art Center College of Design / DESIGNER: Earl Gee / ART DIRECTOR: Earl Gee
661: COMPANY: Jon Flaming Design / CLIENT: Urbana Communities / DESIGNER: Jon Flaming / ART DIRECTOR: Jon Flaming
662: COMPANY: The Joe Bosack Graphic Design Co. / DESIGNER: Joe Bosack / ART DIRECTOR: Joe Bosack

663

664

665

666

667

668

669

670

**663:** COMPANY: Baji Group / CLIENT: When I Go Deaf / DESIGNER: Jonny Ashcroft
**664:** COMPANY: Spindletop Design / CLIENT: Fat Cat Creamery / DESIGNERS: Jennifer Blanco, Tyler Swanner / ART DIRECTOR: Jennifer Blanco
**665:** COMPANY: Thrillustrate / CLIENT: Kids Outreach
**666:** COMPANY: J Sayles Design Co. / CLIENT: Beaverdale Neighborhood / DESIGNER: John Sayles / ART DIRECTOR: John Sayles
**667:** COMPANY: The Joe Bosack Graphic Design Co. / CLIENT: / DESIGNER: Joe Bosack / ART DIRECTOR: Joe Bosack
**668:** COMPANY: DEI Creative / CLIENT: Holland Residential / DESIGNERS: Noah Bell, Maddy Porter / ART DIRECTOR: Sara Green
**669:** COMPANY: Roy Smith Design / CLIENT: Personal / DESIGNER: Roy Smith
**670:** COMPANY: Pacey + Pacey Design / CLIENT: Faye Yao / DESIGNER: Michael Pacey / ART DIRECTOR: Robert Pacey

671

672

673

674

675

676

677

678

**671:** COMPANY: Lethcoe Design / CLIENT: MindFire Communications / DESIGNER: Lance Lethcoe
**672:** COMPANY: Student Project / CLIENT: Art Center College of Design, Pasadena, CA / DESIGNER: Oliver Ryan Lo / ART DIRECTOR: Instructor Dan Hoy
**673:** COMPANY: Matt Lehman Studio / CLIENT: Home Foundation / ART DIRECTOR: Sarah Deane Hale
**674:** COMPANY: Timber Design Co. / DESIGNER: Lars Lawson
**675:** COMPANY: Timber Design Co. / DESIGNER: Lars Lawson
**676:** COMPANY: Jajo / CLIENT: Big Brothers Big Sisters of Sedgwick County / DESIGNER: Andrew Stephens / ART DIRECTOR: Steve Randa
**677:** COMPANY: Device / CLIENT: London / DESIGNER: Rian Hughes / ART DIRECTOR: Rian Hughes
**678:** COMPANY: Varsity Mascot Company / CLIENT: Corban University / DESIGNER: Sam Sedor, Ryan Welty / ART DIRECTOR: Dave Adamson

679

680

681

682

683

684

AIRWAVE

685

679: COMPANY: Pollard Design / DESIGNER: Jeff Pollard
680: COMPANY: Mint / CLIENT: Hoo Doo Brewing / DESIGNER: Bryan Danknich / ART DIRECTOR: Mike Calkins
681: COMPANY: Mint / CLIENT: Squeaky Green / DESIGNER: Julia-Anne Bork
682: COMPANY: R&R Partners / CLIENT: Personal / DESIGNER: Randy Heil / ART DIRECTOR: Randy Heil
683: COMPANY: Sean Heisler / CLIENT: The Upstairs Church / DESIGNER: Sean Heisler / ART DIRECTOR: Sean Heisler
684: COMPANY: R&R Partners / CLIENT: New Vista Community / DESIGNER: Randy Heil / ART DIRECTOR: Randy Heil
685: COMPANY: R&R Partners / CLIENT: Airwave / DESIGNER: Randy Heil / ART DIRECTOR: Randy Heil

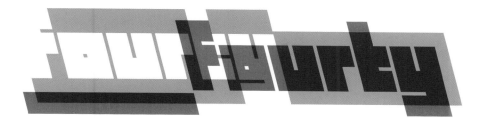

**686**

INFORMONDO

**687**

**688**

**689**

**690**

Salvador Anguiano

**691**

**686:** COMPANY: Device / CLIENT: Fourty Bikes / DESIGNER: Rian Hughes / ART DIRECTOR: Simon Coates
**687:** COMPANY: R&R Partners / CLIENT: R&R Partners / DESIGNER: Randy Heil / ART DIRECTOR: Randy Heil
**688:** COMPANY: R&R Partners / CLIENT: Las Vegas Convention & Visitors Authority / DESIGNER: Randy Heil / ART DIRECTOR: Randy Heil
**689:** COMPANY: Design Center, Inc. / CLIENT: Service Ideas / DESIGNER: Sherwin Schwartzrock / ART DIRECTOR: John Reger
**690:** COMPANY: Device / CLIENT: Jake Kazdall / DESIGNER: Rian Hughes / ART DIRECTOR: Jake Kazdall
**691:** COMPANY: Salvadore Anguiano / CLIENT: Personal Identity / DESIGNER: Salvadore Anguiano / ART DIRECTOR: Salvadore Anguiano

**CATAPULT**

692

Westwood

693

694

695

696

697

mhha

698

INDIAN HARVEST

*Whole Grains, Rice and Legumes*

699

**692:** COMPANY: R&R Partners / CLIENT: Catapult Strategic Design / DESIGNER: Randy Heil / ART DIRECTOR: Randy Heil
**693:** COMPANY: Schwartzrock Graphic Arts / CLIENT: Westwood Lutheran Church / DESIGNER: Sherwin Schwartzrock
**694:** COMPANY: Design Center, Inc. / CLIENT: Target / DESIGNER: Sherwin Schwartzrock / ART DIRECTOR: John Reger
**695:** COMPANY: Schwartzrock Graphic Arts / CLIENT: RiverBrand Design / DESIGNER: Sherwin Schwartzrock
**696:** COMPANY: Tactix Creative, Inc. / CLIENT: Greentree Community / DESIGNER: Paul Howalt
**697:** COMPANY: TY Design / CLIENT: Matuta / DESIGNER: Ty Wilkins / ART DIRECTOR: Ty Wilkins
**698:** COMPANY: Schwartzrock Graphic Arts / CLIENT: MN Health and Housing Association / DESIGNER: Sherwin Schwartzrock
**699:** COMPANY: Schwartzrock Graphic Arts / CLIENT: Initio3i / DESIGNER: Sherwin Schwartzrock

700

**HUNTER HAYES**

701

702

703

704

705

706

707

**700:** COMPANY: Pollard Design / DESIGNER: Jeff Pollard
**701:** COMPANY: Matt Lehman Studio / CLIENT: Warner Music Nashville / ART DIRECTOR: Katherine Petillo
**702:** COMPANY: Schwartzrock Graphic Arts / CLIENT: BI Worldwide / DESIGNER: Sherwin Schwartzrock
**703:** COMPANY: TY Design / CLIENT: Predictobot / DESIGNER: Ty Wilkins / ART DIRECTOR: Ty Wilkins
**704:** COMPANY: Schwartzrock Graphic Arts / CLIENT: Kingstone Media / DESIGNER: Sherwin Schwartzrock
**705:** COMPANY: The Joe Bosack Graphic Design Co. / DESIGNER: Joe Bosack / ART DIRECTOR: Joe Bosack
**706:** COMPANY: Mirko Ilić Corp. / CLIENT: Liberal Democratic Party (Serbia) / DESIGNER: Mirko Ilić / ART DIRECTOR: Mirko Ilić
**707:** COMPANY: Schwartzrock Graphic Arts / CLIENT: RiverBrand Design / DESIGNER: Sherwin Schwartzrock

**FIRM:** RULE29
**DESIGNER / ILLUSTRATOR:** JUSTIN AHRENS
**CLIENT:** TEAM RWB

Team Red, White, and Blue is a grassroots organization that wants to transform the way America supports its wounded veterans when they return from active duty. Team RWB's intention is to create a community of veterans, their families, and American citizens who can enjoy authentic social interaction and shared experiences through activities and events all across America. Rule29 has the privilege of helping Team RWB with strategy and telling their story through print, wearables, environmentals, and through mobile, social media, and web development.

We wanted to create a strong and memorable patriotic mark—one that symbolizes a military focus and something athletes would be proud to wear to help create conversation.

We did endless research on medals, eagles, stars, wings, flags, and all sorts of patriotic iconography. We wanted something strong, unique, and yet parts of it had to be recognizable even at the start. The eagle was bold and the wings and stars came together. Then we added our national colors and everything started to fall into place. It really revealed itself as we worked on it.

*Active, dynamic, and memorable. I like how they simplified the name which makes it far more effective than spelling it out. It keeps it iconic like their brand mark.*

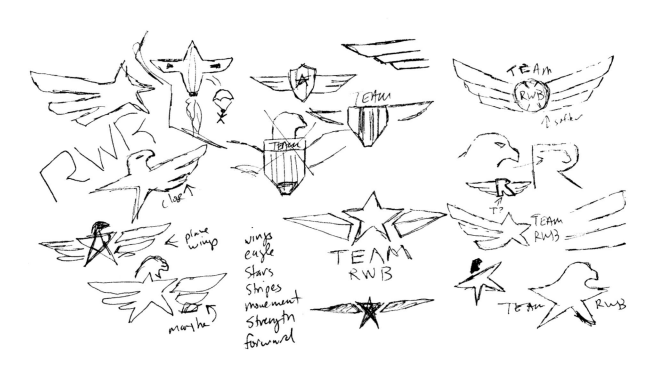

**9.11**

**MEMORIAL RUN**

™

Secondary brand graphics fit into the parent brands aesthetic and work well in the bigger context of promotional efforts for RWB.

 The RWB brand mark is easily applied to a broad range of grassroots uses. Keeping the design easy to use makes the continuity of managing its brand far easier as the organization continues to grow.

708

709

710

TRINITY ELECTRICAL SUPPLY

711

INSOMNIA
ENTERTAINMENT

712

713

714

**708:** COMPANY: Gyula Németh / DESIGNER: Gyula Németh
**709:** COMPANY: Jeremy Slagle Graphic Design / CLIENT: Columbus Brewing Comapny / DESIGNER: Jeremy Slagle / ART DIRECTOR: Jeremy Slagle
**710:** COMPANY: Banowetz & Company / CLIENT: The Trains at NorthPark / DESIGNER: Eric Venegas / ART DIRECTOR: Eric Venegas
**711:** COMPANY: Jon Flaming Design / CLIENT: TESCO / DESIGNER: Jon Flaming / ART DIRECTOR: Jon Flaming
**712:** COMPANY: R&R Partners / CLIENT: Insomnia Entertainment / DESIGNER: Randy Heil / ART DIRECTOR: Randy Heil
**713:** COMPANY: Mode Design / CLIENT: Michael Sanchez / DESIGNER: Hans Bennewitz / ART DIRECTOR: Hans Bennewitz
**714:** COMPANY: J Sayles Design Co. / CLIENT: Beaverdale Neighborhood / DESIGNER: John Sayles / ART DIRECTOR: John Sayles

715

716

717

718

719

720

721

715: COMPANY: Baji Group / CLIENT: Mike Oblinski / DESIGNER: Jonny Ashcroft
716: COMPANY: The Joe Bosack Graphic Design Co. / DESIGNER: Joe Bosack / ART DIRECTOR: Joe Bosack
717: COMPANY: Logo Planet Laboratory / CLIENT: Social Butterfly / DESIGNER: Jeffrey Mardis
718: COMPANY: The Joe Bosack Graphic Design Co. / DESIGNER: Joe Bosack / ART DIRECTOR: Joe Bosack
719: COMPANY: Jon Flaming Design / CLIENT: Helen Houp / DESIGNER: Jon Flaming / ART DIRECTOR: Jon Flaming
720: COMPANY: The Joe Bosack Graphic Design Co. / DESIGNER: Joe Bosack / ART DIRECTOR: Joe Bosack
721: COMPANY: atomicvibe / CLIENT: Steep This! / DESIGNER: Jon Stapp / ART DIRECTOR: Jon Stapp

722

723

724

725

726

727

728

729

**722:** COMPANY: Varsity Mascot Company / CLIENT: Kalapuya Elementary School / DESIGNERS: Sam Sedor, Ryan Welty / ART DIRECTOR: Dave Adamson
**723:** CLIENT: Playa Azul / DESIGNER: Paul Howalt
**724:** COMPANY: R&R Partners / CLIENT: R&R Partners / DESIGNER: Randy Heil / ART DIRECTOR: Randy Heil
**725:** COMPANY: Weather Control / CLIENT: Zumiez / DESIGNER: Josh Oakley
**726:** COMPANY: Schwartzrock Graphic Arts / CLIENT: Freshwater Church / DESIGNER: Sherwin Schwartzrock
**727:** COMPANY: R&R Partners / CLIENT: Harrah's Entertainment / DESIGNER: Randy Heil / ART DIRECTOR: Randy Heil
**728:** COMPANY: R&R Partners / CLIENT: Liquor.com / DESIGNER: Randy Heil / ART DIRECTOR: Randy Heil
**729:** COMPANY: Glitschka Studios / CLIENT: Motto Agency / DESIGNER: Von Glitschka / ART DIRECTOR: Sunny Bonnell

730

# BRITISH AMERICAN
### HOUSEHOLD STAFFING

731

732

733

734

735

736

737

730: COMPANY: leightonhubbell.com / CLIENT: Tiddlywinks Toys and Games / DESIGNER: Leighton Hubbell / ART DIRECTOR: Leighton Hubbell
731: COMPANY: Knoed Creative / CLIENT: BAHS / DESIGNERS: Kim Knoll, Kyle Eertmoed / ART DIRECTOR: Kim Knoll, Kyle Eertmoed
732: COMPANY: Pollard Design / DESIGNER: Jeff Pollard
733: COMPANY: Mint / CLIENT: Urban Freedom / DESIGNER: Mike Calkins
734: COMPANY: J Sayles Design Co. / CLIENT: Des Moines Marathon / DESIGNER: John Sayles / ART DIRECTOR: John Sayles
735: COMPANY: R&R Partners / CLIENT: Ron Lopez / DESIGNER: Randy Heil / ART DIRECTOR: Randy Heil
736: COMPANY: Invisible Creature / CLIENT: Superhero Artist Management / DESIGNER: Ryan Clark / ART DIRECTOR: Ryan Clark
737: CLIENT: BTBG.ru/it-development / DESIGNER: Artem Dvorzhak

**SPACE MONKEY**
STUDIOS INC.

738

739

**METRON**
PRESS

741

740

743

744

738: COMPANY: Invisible Creature / CLIENT: Space Monkey Studios / DESIGNER: Ryan Clark / ART DIRECTOR: Ryan Clark
739: COMPANY: Weather Control / CLIENT: Zumiez / DESIGNER: Josh Oakley
740: COMPANY: R&R Partners / CLIENT: Academy of Hospitality & Tourism / DESIGNER: Randy Heil / ART DIRECTOR: Randy Heil
741: COMPANY: Schwartzrock Graphic Arts / CLIENT: American Bible Society / DESIGNER: Sherwin Schwartzrock
742: COMPANY: R&R Partners / CLIENT: Arizona Chamber of Commerce / DESIGNER: Randy Heil / ART DIRECTOR: Randy Heil
743: COMPANY: R&R Partners / CLIENT: 1SweetLife.org / DESIGNER: Randy Heil / ART DIRECTOR: Randy Heil
744: COMPANY: R&R Partners / CLIENT: Las Vegas Convention & Visitors Authority / DESIGNER: Randy Heil / ART DIRECTOR: Randy Heil

# Bikini

745

746

748

747

749

750

**745:** COMPANY: R&R Partners / CLIENT: Las Vegas Convention & Visitors Authority / DESIGNER: Randy Heil / ART DIRECTOR: Randy Heil
**746:** COMPANY: The Joe Bosack Graphic Design Co. / DESIGNER: Joe Bosack / ART DIRECTOR: Joe Bosack
**747:** COMPANY: Schwartzrock Graphic Arts / CLIENT: BI Worldwide / DESIGNER: Sherwin Schwartzrock
**748:** COMPANY: Schwartzrock Graphic Arts / CLIENT: BI Worldwide / DESIGNER: Sherwin Schwartzrock
**749:** COMPANY: Schwartzrock Graphic Arts / CLIENT: Design Center / DESIGNER: Sherwin Schwartzrock
**750:** COMPANY: R&R Partners / CLIENT: Las Vegas Convention & Visitors Authority / DESIGNER: Randy Heil / ART DIRECTOR: Randy Heil

A NATION IN
MOTION

ONE PATIENT AT A TIME

751

ESTD 1994
SNOWMAN
MECHANICAL

752

BIG ISLAND
INVITATIONAL

753

THE HOUSE
MODESTO

754

755

WINDY CITY
BRAWLERS

756

BH
BUTLER HANSEN
PC

757

AMCOM
SOFTWARE

758

751: COMPANY: Schwartzrock Graphic Arts / CLIENT: RiverBrand Design / DESIGNER: Sherwin Schwartzrock
752: COMPANY: Funnel Design Group / CLIENT: Snowman Mechanical / DESIGNER: Taylor Goad
753: COMPANY: Star Group / CLIENT: AMNRL / DESIGNER: Scott Oeschger / ART DIRECTOR: Scott Oeschger
754: COMPANY: Schwartzrock Graphic Arts / CLIENT: Worlds of Wow / DESIGNER: Sherwin Schwartzrock
755: COMPANY: Schwartzrock Graphic Arts / CLIENT: Frederick and Froberg Design / DESIGNER: Sherwin Schwartzrock
756: COMPANY: Tortoiseshell Black / CLIENT: Windy City Brawlers / DESIGNER: Andy Hall
757: CLIENT: Butler Hansen / DESIGNER: Cam Stewart
758: COMPANY: Schwartzrock Graphic Arts / CLIENT: Hendlin! / DESIGNER: Sherwin Schwartzrock

### HARPER WEST
INSTRUMENT STRINGS

759

### ALCHEMIC
MARKETING CONSULTANTS

760

761

### Blackwood
MANAGEMENT GROUP

762

### aventa
specialized women's care

763

### BAUVOLT

764

### CASTLE
FURNITURE

765

766

759: COMPANY: Hayes Image / CLIENT: Harper West / DESIGNER: Josh Hayes
760: COMPANY: Hayes Image / CLIENT: Alchemic / DESIGNER: Josh Hayes
761: COMPANY: Glischka Studios / CLIENT: Motto Agency / DESIGNER: Von Glitschka / ART DIRECTOR: Sunny Bonnell
762: COMPANY: Schwartzrock Graphic Arts / CLIENT: Blackwood Management Group / DESIGNER: Sherwin Schwartzrock
763: COMPANY: idgroup / CLIENT: Aventa / DESIGNER: Jared Granger / ART DIRECTOR: Gail Sprull-Shaw
764: COMPANY: ACTUART LP. / CLIENT: Bluhm Partner AG / DESIGNER: Peter Vasvari / ART DIRECTOR: Peter Vasvari
765: COMPANY: Tactix Creative, Inc. / CLIENT: Castle Furniture / DESIGNER: Cam Stewart
766: COMPANY: Nissen Design / CLIENT: Music / DESIGNER: John Nissen / ART DIRECTOR: John Nissen

# A Closer Look

**FIRM:** LEIGHTONHUBBELL.COM
**DESIGNER / ILLUSTRATOR:** LEIGHTON HUBBELL
**CLIENTS:** BRADY MACDONALD & WILL HARE

Initially started as a monthly get-together to share and taste new beers, Avocadoville eventually evolved into a combination of good music, spirits, and lively conversation—all in the shade of a century-old Avocado tree.

The design of the logo pays homage to the venue located in Old Towne Orange, California. Historically, the city of Orange is known for its citrus orchards, packing houses, old-growth trees, and community preservation, with many homes built before 1920.

In an effort to stay true to these influences, the logo design uses elements and fonts that lean toward the retro and vintage styles.

*An appropriate design is like a well-tailored suit. It's a comfortable fit and functions well. This logo works well for this client and the intended audience.*

*This fun, conceptual twist on the primary logo is a great secondary brand graphic that is immediately inviting and plays off the curious nature behind the premise of this client's endeavors.*

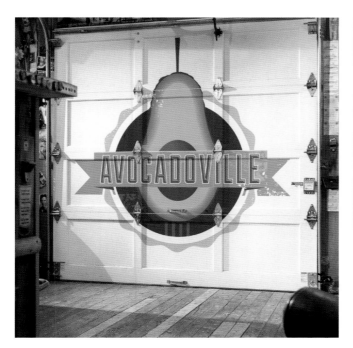

*The application of the new identity to the interior side of the door and its simplified use on barware and coasters really creates a wonderfully captivating presence for those interacting with this business.*

767

768

769

770

771

772

773

767: COMPANY: Eleven19 Communications Inc. / CLIENT: 36 Point / DESIGNER: Ben Lueders / ART DIRECTOR: Donovan Beery
768: COMPANY: Logo Planet Laboratory / CLIENT: Revolution Ice Pops / DESIGNER: Jeffrey Mardis
769: COMPANY: J Sayles Design Co. / DESIGNER: John Sayles / ART DIRECTOR: John Sayles
770: COMPANY: idgroup / CLIENT: Big Brothers Big Sisters / DESIGNER: Jared Granger / ART DIRECTOR: Jared Granger
771: COMPANY: Hatch Design / CLIENT: SF Vinter's Market / DESIGNER: Jeffrey Bucholtz / ART DIRECTORS: Joel Templin, Katie Jain
772: COMPANY: Eleven19 Communications Inc. / CLIENT: Eleven19 Communications Inc. / DESIGNER: Ben Lueders / ART DIRECTOR: Donovan Beery
773: COMPANY: Jon Flaming Design / CLIENT: Pure & Noble / DESIGNER: Jon Flaming / ART DIRECTOR: Jon Flaming

774

775

776

777

MittRomney

778

779

780

774: COMPANY: Eleven19 Communications Inc. / CLIENT: Eleven19 Communications Inc. / DESIGNER: Nicole Blauw / ART DIRECTOR: Donovan Beery
775: COMPANY: Green Ideals / CLIENT: Wiegel Law Group / DESIGNER: Clint G. Delapaz / ART DIRECTOR: Susan Bierzychudek
776: COMPANY: Derek Yoder / CLIENT: The Sparks Family / DESIGNER: Derek Yoder / ART DIRECTOR: Derek Yoder
777: COMPANY: Gardner Design / CLIENT: Chapada Chophouse and Churrascaria / DESIGNER: Brian Miller / ART DIRECTOR: Brian Miller
778: COMPANY: Schwartzrock Graphic Arts / CLIENT: Nobel Communications / DESIGNER: Sherwin Schwartzrock
779: COMPANY: J Sayles Design Co. / CLIENT: Black Diamond / DESIGNER: John Sayles / ART DIRECTOR: John Sayles
780: COMPANY: Hayes Image / CLIENT: Victorian Dept. of Education / DESIGNER: Josh Hayes

781

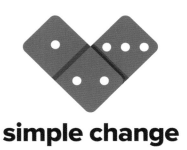

**simple change**

782

783

784

785

786

787

CHRISTIAN
CARPENTRY

788

**781:** COMPANY: The Joe Bosack Graphic Design Co. / DESIGNER: Joe Bosack / ART DIRECTOR: Joe Bosack
**782:** COMPANY: Baji Group / CLIENT: The Urban Child Institute / DESIGNER: Jonny Ashcroft / ART DIRECTOR: Josh Horton
**783:** COMPANY: Fernandez Studio / CLIENT: NHTSA / DESIGNER: Carlos Fernandez / ART DIRECTOR: Brian Potter
**784:** COMPANY: The Joe Bosack Graphic Design Co. / DESIGNER: Joe Bosack / ART DIRECTOR: Joe Bosack
**785:** COMPANY: Gardner Design / CLIENT: Jump Startle / DESIGNER: Luke Bott / ART DIRECTOR: Brian Miller
**786:** COMPANY: The Joe Bosack Graphic Design Co. / DESIGNER: Joe Bosack / ART DIRECTOR: Joe Bosack
**787:** COMPANY: J Sayles Design Co. / CLIENT: Des Moines Marathon / DESIGNER: John Sayles / ART DIRECTOR: John Sayles
**788:** COMPANY: Adam Anderson / DESIGNER: Adam Anderson

789

790

791

792

793

794

795

796

**789:** COMPANY: The Joe Bosack Graphic Design Co. / DESIGNER: Joe Bosack / ART DIRECTOR: Joe Bosack
**790:** COMPANY: Fernandez Studio / CLIENT: Phillips Acquisitons / DESIGNER: Carlos Fernandez / ART DIRECTOR: Carlos Fernandez
**791:** COMPANY: Jon Flaming Design / CLIENT: Watermark Community Church / DESIGNER: Jon Flaming / ART DIRECTOR: Jon Flaming
**792:** COMPANY: Gyula Németh / DESIGNER: Gyula Németh
**793:** COMPANY: J Sayles Design Co. / CLIENT: Winterset Bike Night / DESIGNER: John Sayles / ART DIRECTOR: John Sayles
**794:** COMPANY: The Joe Bosack Graphic Design Co. / DESIGNER: Joe Bosack / ART DIRECTOR: Joe Bosack
**795:** COMPANY: Flight Deck Creative / CLIENT: Texas Frightmare Weekend / DESIGNER: Jason Rahn / ART DIRECTOR: Jason Rahn
**796:** COMPANY: leightonhubbell.com / CLIENT: Hollywood Games / DESIGNER: Leighton Hubbell / ART DIRECTOR: Leighton Hubbell

797

798

799

SAM VILLA

800

801

802

FANADDICT

803

**797:** COMPANY: Michael Doret Graphic Design / CLIENT: Storyville Post / DESIGNER: Michael Doret / ART DIRECTOR: Mark Pruett
**798:** COMPANY: R&R Partners / CLIENT: Personal Work / DESIGNER: Randy Heil / ART DIRECTOR: Randy Heil
**799:** COMPANY: Catapult Strategic Design / CLIENT: Allied Waste / DESIGNER: Randy Heil / ART DIRECTOR: Randy Heil
**800:** COMPANY: R&R Partners / CLIENT: Sam Villa / DESIGNER: Randy Heil / ART DIRECTOR: Randy Heil
**801:** COMPANY: TY Design / CLIENT: Taylor Griswold / DESIGNER: Ty Wilkins / ART DIRECTOR: Ty Wilkins
**802:** COMPANY: Schwartzrock Graphic Arts / CLIENT: Target / DESIGNER: Sherwin Schwartzrock
**803:** COMPANY: REACTOR design Studio / CLIENT: Fan Addict / DESIGNER: Julie Sebby / ART DIRECTORS: Chase Wilson, Clifton Alexander

# SHOPTALKS

**804**

**805**

**807**

**806**

**808**

**809**

**804:** COMPANY: Ramp / CLIENT: AIGA Los Angeles / DESIGNER: Michael Stinson / ART DIRECTOR: Michael Stinson
**805:** COMPANY: Invisible Creature / CLIENT: Invisible Creature / DESIGNER: Don Clark / ART DIRECTOR: Don Clark
**806:** COMPANY: chameleon design / CLIENT: Caio Ferracioli / DESIGNER: Tomas Vateha / ART DIRECTOR: Tomas Vateha
**807:** COMPANY: J Sayles Design Co. / CLIENT: Metro Arts / DESIGNER: John Sayles / ART DIRECTOR: John Sayles
**808:** COMPANY: Timber Design Co. / DESIGNER: Lars Lawson
**809:** CLIENT: http://vikiland.ru// / DESIGNER: Artem Dvorzhak

810

811

812

813

814

815

816

817

**810:** COMPANY: R&R Partners / CLIENT: R&R Partners / DESIGNER: Randy Heil / ART DIRECTOR: Randy Heil
**811:** COMPANY: Schwartzrock Graphic Arts / CLIENT: Partnership for Strong Families / DESIGNER: Sherwin Schwartzrock
**812:** COMPANY: Hayes Image / CLIENT: Matthew Clemmons / DESIGNER: Josh Hayes
**813:** COMPANY: Hayes Image / CLIENT: Rhythm Magical / DESIGNER: Josh Hayes
**814:** COMPANY: Throttle Design Mechanics / CLIENT: Ron Heagy / DESIGNER: Wendel Hayes, Dave Adamson / ART DIRECTOR: Dave Adamson
**815:** COMPANY: R&R Partners / CLIENT: NV Energy / DESIGNER: Randy Heil / ART DIRECTOR: Randy Heil
**816:** COMPANY: Schwartzrock Graphic Arts / CLIENT: BI Worldwide / DESIGNER: Sherwin Schwartzrock
**817:** COMPANY: Schwartzrock Graphic Arts / CLIENT: Frederick and Froberg Design / DESIGNER: Sherwin Schwartzrock

819

820

822

JOHN & SANDRA

REGER

821

823

824

RANDY
BRALEY
PHOTOGRAPHY

825

818: COMPANY: R&R Partners / CLIENT: Pete Ernaut / DESIGNER: Randy Heil / ART DIRECTOR: Randy Heil
819: COMPANY: R&R Partners / CLIENT: Las Vegas Convention & Visitors Authority / DESIGNER: Randy Heil / ART DIRECTOR: Randy Heil
820: COMPANY: Schwartzrock Graphic Arts / CLIENT: Target / DESIGNER: Sherwin Schwartzrock / ART DIRECTOR: Sherwin Schwartzrock
822: COMPANY: Schwartzrock Graphic Arts / CLIENT: Design Center / DESIGNER: Sherwin Schwartzrock
823: COMPANY: R&R Partners / CLIENT: Lee Horswell / DESIGNER: Randy Heil / ART DIRECTOR: Randy Heil
824: COMPANY: Schwartzrock Graphic Arts / CLIENT: BI Worldwide / DESIGNER: Sherwin Schwartzrock
825: COMPANY: REACTOR design Studio / CLIENT: Randy Braley Photography / DESIGNER: Chase Wilson / ART DIRECTOR: Clifton Alexander

**FIRM:** LUKE BOTT
**DESIGNER / ILLUSTRATOR:** LUKE BOTT
**ART DIRECTOR:** LUKE BOTT
**CLIENT:** AMR SOBHY, PUSHBOTS INC.

In PushBots, we help mobile developers talk to their customers and increase loyalty and meaningful growth with a minimum amount of resources. PushBots is a service that helps mobile developers minimize the time and resources required to keep their users engaged with their apps by making highly personalized content according to their interest easier than ever. This is like when Facebook notifies a user after somebody wrote something on his or her wall.

PushBots helps developers focus on the real development of their app, instead of struggling with code and complex protocols, not to mention the time spent on servers and infrastructure. Worrying about scalability, growth, and extending an app to other platforms is eliminated. We do that work for developers all while tracking the success and growth of their app.

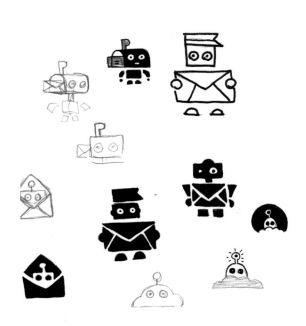

*This project could very well have ended up being a complete yawner. Code author clients I've known have a tendency to get wrapped up in technical minutia and are not always the most visually literate bunch. However, Bott has managed to infuse maximum amounts of personality into his client's identity. These two logo directions alone communicate marvelously with just the perfect amount of detail.*

*These vibrant and playful spot diagrams and characters further establish the client's fun-loving personality. The flat graphic style complements the simple geometric shapes of the robot characters perfectly. I almost want to plop down on the couch in my PJs with a bowl of cereal and enjoy them like I was a kid watching his favorite animated special.*

THE **FUTURE** OF MOBILE MESSAGING

*This is a gorgeous palette selection. This style guide is a beautiful departure from the sterile visual world we expect from tech companies like this.*

826

**CoffeeChat**

827

**FiESTA**

829

828

830

single parent family

831

832

826: COMPANY: The Joe Bosack Graphic Design Co. / DESIGNER: Joe Bosack / ART DIRECTOR: Joe Bosack
827: COMPANY: chameleon design / CLIENT: Milles Ray / DESIGNER: Tomas Vateha / ART DIRECTOR: Tomas Vateha
828: COMPANY: Brent Couchman Design / CLIENT: Zeus Jones, Nordstrom / DESIGNER: Brent Couchman / ART DIRECTOR: Brad Surcey
829: COMPANY: Greteman Group / CLIENT: City of Wichita / DESIGNER: Chris Parks / ART DIRECTOR: Sonia Greteman
830: COMPANY: Jared Granger / CLIENT: Dane Digital Vision / DESIGNER: Jared Granger / ART DIRECTOR: Jared Granger
831: COMPANY: Jon Flaming Design / CLIENT: Watermark Community Church / DESIGNER: Jon Flaming / ART DIRECTOR: Jon Flaming
832: COMPANY: Hatch Design / CLIENT: Segrams / DESIGNER: Eszter Clark / ART DIRECTORS: Joel Templin, Katie Jain

833

uberri
fashion conscious

834

835

FALCON WHITE
DESIGNAGENTUR

836

ChurchShield

837

JARED JONES
Financial Wellness

838

watermark**arts**

839

**833:** COMPANY: Banowetz & Company / CLIENT: St John's Episcopal School / DESIGNER: Sarah Terrell / ART DIRECTOR: Eric Venegas
**834:** COMPANY: Hayes Image / CLIENT: Uberri / DESIGNER: Josh Hayes
**835:** COMPANY: ACTUART LP / CLIENT: TWOEWE / DESIGNER: Peter Vasvari / ART DIRECTOR: Peter Vasvari
**836:** COMPANY: Falcon White / CLIENT: Falcon White / DESIGNER: Kerstin Krause, Ralf Krause / ART DIRECTORS: Kerstin Krause, Ralf Krause
**837:** COMPANY: Miles Design / CLIENT: ChurchShield / DESIGNER: Brian K. Gray
**838:** COMPANY: Jared Granger / CLIENT: Jared Jones / DESIGNER: Jared Granger / ART DIRECTOR: Jared Granger
**839:** COMPANY: Jon Flaming Design / CLIENT: Watermark Community Church / DESIGNER: Jon Flaming / ART DIRECTOR: Jon Flaming

840

841

842

843

844

845

846

847

**840:** COMPANY: J Sayles Design Co. , CLIENT: Jordan River / DESIGNER: John Sayles / ART DIRECTOR: John Sayles
**841:** COMPANY: Schwartzrock Graphic Arts / CLIENT: RiverBrand Design / DESIGNER: Sherwin Schwartzrock
**842:** COMPANY: R&R Partners / CLIENT: Cigna/Care Today / DESIGNER: Randy Heil / ART DIRECTOR: Randy Heil
**843:** COMPANY: leightonhubbell.com / CLIENT: Hollwood Games / DESIGNER: Leighton Hubbell / ART DIRECTOR: Leighton Hubbell
**844:** COMPANY: leightonhubbell.com / CLIENT: Pipeline Digital Media / DESIGNER: Leighton Hubbell / ART DIRECTOR: Leighton Hubbell
**845:** COMPANY: Spindletop Design / CLIENT: Catalina Coffee / DESIGNERS: Jennifer Blanco, Laura Tait, Tyler Swanner / ART DIRECTOR: Jennifer Blanco
**846:** CLIENT: Aziam Brand Identity Development / DESIGNER: U! Creative Team
**847:** COMPANY: leightonhubbell.com / CLIENT: Pipeline Digital Media / DESIGNER: Leighton Hubbell / ART DIRECTOR: Leighton Hubbell

848

849

850

851

852

853

854

855

**848:** COMPANY: Kris Bazen Creative / CLIENT: Houston Roller Derby Valkyries, Houston, TX / DESIGNER: Kris Bazen / ART DIRECTOR: Kris Bazen
**849:** COMPANY: Kris Bazen Creative / CLIENT: Manasseas High School Tigers, Memphis, TN / DESIGNER: Kris Bazen / ART DIRECTOR: Kris Bazen
**850:** COMPANY: Gravitate Design Studio / DESIGNER: Marc Neidlinger / ART DIRECTOR: Marc Neidlinger
**851:** COMPANY: REACTOR design Studio / CLIENT: DekTile Concrete Overlays / DESIGNER: Patrick Drake, Samantha Fine / ART DIRECTOR: Clifton Alexander, Chase Wilson
**852:** COMPANY: Roy Smith Design / CLIENT: Kallaway / DESIGNER: Roy Smith
**853:** COMPANY: Spindletop Design / CLIENT: Workhorse Printmakers / DESIGNER: Jennifer Blance, John Earles / ART DIRECTOR: Jennifer Blanco
**854:** COMPANY: Pollard Design / DESIGNER: Jeff Pollard
**855:** COMPANY: U! Creative, Inc. / CLIENT: E3 / DESIGNER: U! Creative Team

856

857

858

859

860

861

862

856: COMPANY: Weather Control / CLIENT: Ms. Taken / DESIGNER: Josh Oakley
857: COMPANY: Jared Granger / CLIENT: Exploration / DESIGNER: Jared Granger / ART DIRECTOR: Jared Granger
858: COMPANY: Miles Design / CLIENT: Global Health Systems / DESIGNER: Brian K. Gray
860: COMPANY: Throttle Design Mechanics / CLIENT: Throttle Design Mechanics / DESIGNER: John Nissen / ART DIRECTOR: Dave Adamson
861: COMPANY: Invisible Creature / CLIENT: Fixcraft / DESIGNER: Ryan Clark / ART DIRECTOR: Ryan Clark
862: COMPANY: Mint / CLIENT: Blue Jay Productions / DESIGNER: Mike Calkins
862: COMPANY: Varsity Mascot Company / CLIENT: Battle Creek Elementary School / DESIGNER: Sam Sedor, Ryan Welty / ART DIRECTOR: Dave Adamson

863

864

**Banjo Cat**

865

866

867

868

863: COMPANY: Jared Granger / CLIENT: Exploration / DESIGNER: Jared Granger / ART DIRECTOR: Jared Granger
864: COMPANY: Mint / CLIENT: Buck Knives / DESIGNER: Mike Calkins
865: COMPANY: R&R Partners / CLIENT: Airwave / DESIGNER: Randy Heil / ART DIRECTOR: Randy Heil
866: COMPANY: Touchwood Design Inc. / CLIENT: GreenFuse Photography / DESIGNER: Shawn Murenbeeld / ART DIRECTOR: Shawn Murenbeeld
867: COMPANY: Jeff Andrews Design / CLIENT: / DESIGNER: Jeff Andrews / ART DIRECTOR: Jeff Andrews
868: COMPANY: Mint / CLIENT: Gift / DESIGNER: Mike Calkins

**SHERPA PICTURES**

869

## SEN5E

870

**A PARK
CITIES DINER**

871

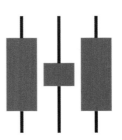

872

873

the Quarter

874

*A király liliomja*
ESKÜVŐI RUHA SZALON

875

**TERRAMARKER**™

876

**869:** COMPANY: R&R Partners / CLIENT: Sherpa / DESIGNER: Randy Heil / ART DIRECTOR: Randy Heil
**870:** COMPANY: Shawn Meek / CLIENT: SENSE / DESIGNER: Shawn Meek
**871:** COMPANY: Banowetz & Company / CLIENT: The Front Room / DESIGNER: Eric Venegas / ART DIRECTOR: Eric Venegas
**872:** COMPANY: Joseph Blalock Design Office / CLIENT: MTV/Hype / DESIGNER: Joseph Blalock
**873:** COMPANY: Schwartzrock Graphic Arts / CLIENT: Freshwater Church / DESIGNER: Sherwin Schwartzrock
**874:** COMPANY: Schwartzrock Graphic Arts / CLIENT: Tim Westermeyer / DESIGNER: Sherwin Schwartzrock
**875:** COMPANY: Voov Ltd. / CLIENT: Ginapron Ltd. / DESIGNER: Tunde Varga / ART DIRECTOR: Balint Egyed
**876:** CLIENT: TerraMarker / DESIGNER: Julian Hrankov

PRODUCTION

MUSIC

877

878

879

880

881

Take Your Place

882

883

884

877: COMPANY: Joseph Blalock Design Office / CLIENT: MTV/Hype / DESIGNER: Joseph Blalock
878: DESIGNER: Floris Voorveld / ART DIRECTOR: Floris Voorveld
879: COMPANY: Tactix Creative, Inc. / CLIENT: Vianet / DESIGNER: Paul Howalt
880: COMPANY: Schwartzrock Graphic Arts / CLIENT: BI Worldwide / DESIGNER: Sherwin Schwartzrock
881: COMPANY: Varsity Mascot Company / CLIENT: Salem Academy High School / DESIGNER: Sam Sedor, Wendel Hayes / ART DIRECTOR: Dave Adamson
882: COMPANY: Touchwood Design Inc. / CLIENT: Public Inc. / DESIGNER: Shawn Murenbeeld / ART DIRECTOR: Shawn Murenbeeld
883: COMPANY: Design Nut / CLIENT: Piper Watson Photography / DESIGNER: Brent M. Almond / ART DIRECTOR: Brent M. Almond
884: COMPANY: Joseph Blalock Design Office / CLIENT: MTV/Hype / DESIGNER: Joseph Blalock

*a*   *b*

# 25 Years of Logo Design, Distilled

SHERWIN SCHWARTZROCK

I started my career in 1988, and since then, I've been fortunate enough to create hundreds of corporate identities and logos. I've worked in the precomputer world with ink, rubilith, and stat cameras and seen the industry transformed by clip art logo websites and most recently, a logo design software package for $40 (£26). A lot has changed in the past twenty-five years, and I've seen the corporate brands of the world go from the simple, to the complex, to the 3-D, to the animated, to the simple again. All of this has formed my opinions about logo design.

## 1. I don't create clip art logos anymore.

What is a clip art logo? It's a logo symbol that if you switch out the company name, can be used for any company. In the past, I've created hundreds of them. Before the popularity of clip art logo sites, I was guilty of repackaging logos created for past clients (that were not chosen) and reselling them to new clients. Lots of companies use these marks, but it isn't optimum. If another company could reuse your logo icon, that mark isn't unique—and what does that say about your company?

## 2. Acronyms are usually worthless.

Ever since IBM, everyone feels a three-letter ancronym is the industry norm. But, what do three letters mean to anyone who isn't familiar with the company? Nothing. And, in the case of brands we are familiar with, they lose that meaning over time. Does anyone under thirty know that IBM stands for International Business Machines? That CBS stands for Columbia Broadcasting System? Those brands have given personality to their three letters over time. But for a new company, it simply doesn't add value (fig. a, b).

c

d

e

f

### 3. I design more logotypes today.
In the past, I almost never created wordmarks, though I'm not sure why. I think designers have something against them because they don't highlight design skills in as obvious a manner. The truth is they are easier to use across different applications because they require less rules to implement. Still, let me just say, I don't believe in "just type" treatments unless they are built from custom typography. The font choice does say a lot about a company, but visually, I believe there needs to be something more than just type to be memorable (fig. c, d).

In the last decade or more, you've seen companies move toward shorter names, which makes a logotype possible. Amazon, Yahoo, and Google are just a few success stories.

### 4. Have a good roadmap.
How do you know if you've created the perfect logo? Know what it should do, before you go about creating it. So often logo design begins as an art project and not a communications project. Save yourself time and make more effective work by clearly defining the goals of your brand.

### 5. Get to the point.
In today's marketplace, there is so much visual clutter, the consumer doesn't have much time to figure out who you are and what you're selling. Brands need to define their product and position in the marketplace as quickly as possible. This means everything in a brand identity has to pull its weight. Now, more than ever, refinement from the company name to the visual aesthetics is scrutinized.

I'll use the Initio3i logo as an example. Initially, I designed this mark for Initio Advertising (fig. e, top). I started by creating a custom typeface, then I added a unique element to it that focused on the major change in our industry: Instead of broadcasting messages to the masses, clients through advertising communicate one-to-one with their audience. Great! Later, the company split into two legal entities and the "3i" was added to the mark (fig e, bottom). Not so great, but we lived with it for awhile. Finally, realizing that the personality and position of the new company now revolved around the definition of 3i, we refined the same concept into a simpler, more memorable mark. Not an ideal process, but we found success in spite of it (fig. f).

### 6. Environment is king.
This truth has never changed. I was taught this in school and it's still true today. Consider the primary point of contact where your consumers interact with the brand. Build the mark to fit that environment. Some marks require flexibility, where others can leverage their exclusive real estate. A logo that lives exclusively on a website, phone, or tablet has different considerations than a mark that is embroidered on denim.

### 7. Don't be an artist.
Finally, I would like to give all of the logo designers in the world this piece of advice: If you are an artist, get out of this business. Let me give some context. I define an artist as someone who has a voice, and they create work that conveys that voice. Graphic designers aren't artists, they are communicators. A communicator projects the voice of the client. It's very easy in this profession to mix up the two. Too often we forget that our visual preference does not outweigh the needs of our clients. Don't make that mistake.

# Logo Gallery

885

886

# FIRST PRES

**FIRST PRESBYTERIAN CHURCH**

FORT LAUDERDALE, FL • EST. 1942

887

888

888

889

890

891

885: COMPANY: Sevenfiles / CLIENT: Restaurante Natalia / DESIGNER: Carlos Ribeiro / ART DIRECTOR: Carlos Ribeiro
886: COMPANY: Glischka Studios / CLIENT: Street Level / DESIGNER: Von Glitschka / ART DIRECTOR: Lisa Duty
887: COMPANY: atomicvibe / CLIENT: First Presbyterian Church of Fort Lauderdale / DESIGNER: Jon Stapp / ART DIRECTOR: Jon Stapp
888: COMPANY: Gyula Németh / DESIGNER: Gyula Németh
889: COMPANY: Greteman Group / CLIENT: Botanica Gardens / DESIGNER: Chris Parks / ART DIRECTOR: Sonia Greteman
890: COMPANY: Adam Anderson / DESIGNER: Adam Anderson
891: COMPANY: Derek Yoder / CLIENT: Garfield Middle School / DESIGNER: Derek Yoder / ART DIRECTOR: Derek Yoder

892

893

894

895

MIRAVISTA

896

897

898

**892:** COMPANY: Gyula Németh / DESIGNER: Gyula Németh
**893:** COMPANY: Derek Yoder / CLIENT: The Stirrup Project / DESIGNER: Joshua Jenniges / ART DIRECTOR: Derek Yoder
**894:** COMPANY: Fluxar Studios / CLIENT: The Mark / DESIGNER: Hans Bennewitz / ART DIRECTOR: Kynan Chambers
**895:** COMPANY: The Joe Bosack Graphic Design Co. / DESIGNER: Joe Bosack / ART DIRECTOR: Joe Bosack
**896:** COMPANY: Jon Flaming Design / CLIENT: Urbana Communities / DESIGNER: Jon Flaming / ART DIRECTOR: Jon Flaming
**897:** COMPANY: Tactix Creative, Inc. / CLIENT: Anderson Concrete / DESIGNER: Paul Howalt
**898:** COMPANY: Gardner Design / CLIENT: Chapada Chophouse and Churrascaria / DESIGNER: Brian Miller / ART DIRECTOR: Brian Miller

899

900

901

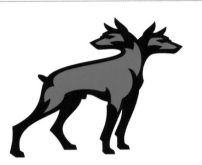

902

903

904

905

906

**899:** COMPANY: Jon Flaming Design / CLIENT: Watermark Community Church / DESIGNER: Jon Flaming / ART DIRECTOR: Jon Flaming
**900:** COMPANY: Pollard Design / DESIGNER: Jeff Pollard
**901:** COMPANY: J Sayles Design Co. / CLIENT: DNR of Iowa / DESIGNER: John Sayles / ART DIRECTOR: John Sayles
**902:** COMPANY: Pollard Design / DESIGNER: Jeff Pollard
**903:** COMPANY: leightonhubbell.com / CLIENT: Outrageous California BBQ / DESIGNER: Leighton Hubbell / ART DIRECTOR: Leighton Hubbell
**904:** COMPANY: leightonhubbell.com / CLIENT: Select Beer Bottle Shop and Tap Room / DESIGNER: Leighton Hubbell / ART DIRECTOR: Leighton Hubbell
**905:** COMPANY: Kris Bazen Creative / CLIENT: Miscellaneous Athletes Concept / DESIGNER: Kris Bazen / ART DIRECTOR: Kris Bazen
**906:** COMPANY: leightonhubbell.com / CLIENT: San Jacinto College / DESIGNER: Leighton Hubbell / ART DIRECTOR: Leighton Hubbell

907

908

909

910

911

913

912

914

907: COMPANY: Student Project / CLIENT: Art Center College of Design, Pasadena, CA / DESIGNER: Oliver Ryan Lo / ART DIRECTOR: Instructor Dan Hoy
908: COMPANY: Michael Doret Graphic Design / CLIENT: NBA / DESIGNER: Michael Doret / ART DIRECTOR: Tom O'Grady
909: COMPANY: leightonhubbell.com / CLIENT: Zuzu's Petals Floral Design / DESIGNER: Leighton Hubbell / ART DIRECTOR: Leighton Hubbell
910: COMPANY: Timber Design Co. / DESIGNER: Lars Lawson
911: COMPANY: Sean Heisler / CLIENT: Bendy You Photography / DESIGNER: Sean Heisler / ART DIRECTOR: Sean Heisler
912: COMPANY: Mirko Ilić Corp. / CLIENT: First Born Films / DESIGNER: Mirko Ilić / ART DIRECTOR: Mirko Ilić
913: COMPANY: J Sayles Design Co. / CLIENT: Tifereth / DESIGNER: John Sayles / ART DIRECTOR: John Sayles
914: COMPANY: REACTOR design studio / CLIENT: National Assoc of Public Charter School / DESIGNER: Chase Wilson, Julie Sebby / ART DIRECTOR: Clifton Alexander

915

916

917

918

919

920

921

**915:** COMPANY: Chase Design Group / CLIENT: Mattel / DESIGNERS: Margo Chase, Clark Goolsby / ART DIRECTOR: Margo Chase
**916:** COMPANY: R&R Partners / CLIENT: Vegas Rock Dog / DESIGNER: Randy Heil / ART DIRECTOR: Randy Heil
**917:** COMPANY: Invisible Creature / CLIENT: Invisible Creature / DESIGNER: Don Clark / ART DIRECTOR: Don Clark
**918:** COMPANY: Mint / CLIENT: American Eagle Outfitters / DESIGNER: Mike Calkins
**919:** COMPANY: R&R Partners / CLIENT: Las Vegas Hilton / DESIGNER: Randy Heil / ART DIRECTOR: Randy Heil
**920:** COMPANY: R&R Partners / CLIENT: Bananafish / DESIGNER: Randy Heil / ART DIRECTOR: Randy Heil
**921:** COMPANY: R&R Partners / CLIENT: MGM Mirage / DESIGNER: Randy Heil / ART DIRECTOR: Randy Heil

## THE RAIL AHEAD

922

923

924

925

the
**GLOBE**

ZURI

926

927

**922:** COMPANY: R&R Partners / CLIENT: Western High-Speed Rail Alliance / DESIGNER: Randy Heil / ART DIRECTOR: Randy Heil
**923:** COMPANY: R&R Partners / CLIENT: Southern Nevada Water Authority / DESIGNER: Randy Heil / ART DIRECTOR: Randy Heil
**924:** COMPANY: Mint / CLIENT: Urban Freedom / DESIGNER: Mike Calkins
**925:** COMPANY: R&R Partners / CLIENT: Dodge's / DESIGNER: Randy Heil / ART DIRECTOR: Randy Heil
**926:** COMPANY: Mattson Creative / DESIGNER: Ty Mattson
**927:** COMPANY: R&R Partners / CLIENT: Hogle Zoo / DESIGNER: Randy Heil / ART DIRECTOR: Randy Heil

# Logo Gallery

928

929

930

931

932

933

934

935

**928:** COMPANY: R&R Partners / CLIENT: Personal / DESIGNER: Randy Heil / ART DIRECTOR: Randy Heil
**929:** COMPANY: Tactix Creative, Inc. / CLIENT: Oomph! Labs Logo / DESIGNER: Paul Howalt
**930:** COMPANY: R&R Partners / CLIENT: R&R Partners / DESIGNER: Randy Heil / ART DIRECTOR: Randy Heil
**931:** COMPANY: Tactix Creative, Inc. / CLIENT: Higley School District / DESIGNER: Paul Howalt
**932:** COMPANY: Voov Ltd. / CLIENT: Kobor Kisgep Szerviz / DESIGNER: Tünde Varga / ART DIRECTOR: Bálint Egyed
**933:** COMPANY: Tactix Creative, Inc. / CLIENT: Payne & Son / DESIGNER: Cam Stewart
**934:** COMPANY: Magnum / CLIENT: Santa Monica Brew Works / DESIGNER: Scott Oeschger / ART DIRECTOR: Scott Oeschger
**935:** COMPANY: Schwartzrock Graphic Arts / CLIENT: BI Worldwide / DESIGNER: Sherwin Schwartzrock

936

937

938

939

940

941

942

943

936: COMPANY: Schwartzrock Graphic Arts / CLIENT: Nobel Communications / DESIGNER: Sherwin Schwartzrock
937: COMPANY: Schwartzrock Graphic Arts / CLIENT: Digital Lake, Inc. / DESIGNER: Sherwin Schwartzrock
938: COMPANY: Schwartzrock Graphic Arts / CLIENT: Kingstone Media / DESIGNER: Sherwin Schwartzrock
939: COMPANY: Schwartzrock Graphic Arts / CLIENT: BI Worldwide / DESIGNER: Sherwin Schwartzrock
940: COMPANY: Schwartzrock Graphic Arts / CLIENT: Yanovick, Inc. / DESIGNER: Sherwin Schwartzrock
941: COMPANY: Schwartzrock Graphic Arts / CLIENT: AMI / DESIGNER: Sherwin Schwartzrock
942: COMPANY: Schwartzrock Graphic Arts / CLIENT: American Bible Society / DESIGNER: Sherwin Schwartzrock
943: COMPANY: Schwartzrock Graphic Arts / CLIENT: Yanovick, Inc. / DESIGNER: Sherwin Schwartzrock

**FIRM:** MINT
**DESIGNER / ILLUSTRATOR:** MIKE CALKINS
**CLIENT:** HILLIARD'S BREWERY

A new artisanal brewery opening in Seattle's Ballard neighborhood warranted a sleek contemporary twist on the vernacular of beer culture. A fresh application of a crisp herringbone pattern balances cleanly executed typography, channeling traditional European blackletter in a contemporary way.

*The strength of this design is its balance of contemporary and classic sensibilities without compromising the authenticity of either.*

*The work Mint produces is extremely well executed and that has a lot to do with their process, thoroughly exploring potential before settling on any one direction. All of these are well-thought-out and played a part in shaping the overall direction.*

Mint has positioned this new company with a brand on par with a multinational. The final product and its application is beautiful and will help equip a young company in their marketing efforts at every level.

944

945

WELLNESS
W A R R I O R

946

CCAD**MIND**SHOP

947

948

949

K A N S A S
AVIATION
M U S E U M

950

**944:** COMPANY: Adam Anderson / DESIGNER: Adam Anderson
**945:** COMPANY: atomicvibe / CLIENT: Sweet Toof Bakery / DESIGNER: Jon Stapp / ART DIRECTOR: Jon Stapp
**946:** COMPANY: Greteman Group / CLIENT: Royal Carribean / DESIGNER: Chris Parks / ART DIRECTOR: Sonia Greteman
**947:** COMPANY: Base Art Co. / CLIENT: Columbus College of Art & Design / DESIGNERS: Drue Dixon, Meredith Reuter, Terry Rohrbach / ART DIRECTOR: Terry Rohrbach
**948:** COMPANY: Sevenfiles / CLIENT: Movimento Vaó-se Foder / DESIGNER: Carlos Ribeiro / ART DIRECTOR: Carlos Ribeiro
**949:** COMPANY: Charles Akins, AkinsTudio / CLIENT: Grasshopper Kids Basketball League / DESIGNERS: Charles Akins, AkinsTudio / ART DIRECTORS: Charles Akins, AkinsTudio
**950:** COMPANY: Greteman Group / CLIENT: Kansas Aviation Museum / DESIGNER: Chris Parks / ART DIRECTOR: Sonia Greteman

951

952

953

954

955

PUBLIC ART OMAHA

956

957

**951:** COMPANY: Gyula Németh / DESIGNER: Gyula Németh
**952:** COMPANY: Gardner Design / CLIENT: Scone Woman / DESIGNER: Brian Miller / ART DIRECTOR: Brian Miller
**953:** COMPANY: Greteman Group / CLIENT: Royal Caribbean / DESIGNER: Chris Parks / ART DIRECTOR: Sonia Greteman
**954:** COMPANY: Gardner Design / CLIENT: Pauline Reese / DESIGNER: Brian Miller / ART DIRECTOR: Brian Miller
**955:** COMPANY: Chase Design Group / CLIENT: Target / DESIGNER: Margo Chase / ART DIRECTOR: Margo Chase
**956:** COMPANY: Eleven19 Communications Inc. / CLIENT: Public Art Omaha / DESIGNER: Donovan Beery / ART DIRECTOR: Donovan Beery
**957:** COMPANY: Eleven19 Communications Inc. / CLIENT: Eleven19 Communications Inc. / DESIGNER: Ben Lueders / ART DIRECTOR: Donovan Beery

958

959

960

961

962

963

964

965

**958:** COMPANY: Gyula Németh / DESIGNER: Gyula Németh
**959:** COMPANY: leightonhubbell.com / CLIENT: Leisure Interactive / DESIGNER: Leighton Hubbell / ART DIRECTOR: Leighton Hubbell
**960:** COMPANY: leightonhubbell.com / CLIENT: Leisure Interactive / DESIGNER: Leighton Hubbell / ART DIRECTOR: Leighton Hubbell
**961:** COMPANY: The Joe Bosack Graphic Design Co. / CLIENT: / DESIGNER: Joe Bosack / ART DIRECTOR: Joe Bosack
**962:** COMPANY: leightonhubbell.com / CLIENT: Bancroft School / DESIGNER: Leighton Hubbell / ART DIRECTOR: Leighton Hubbell
**963:** COMPANY: leightonhubbell.com / CLIENT: Avocadoville / DESIGNER: Leighton Hubbell / ART DIRECTOR: Leighton Hubbell
**964:** COMPANY: The Joe Bosack Graphic Design Co. / CLIENT: / DESIGNER: Joe Bosack / ART DIRECTOR: Joe Bosack
**965:** COMPANY: Greteman Group / CLIENT: Real Men, Real Heroes / DESIGNER: Ty Wilkens / ART DIRECTOR: Sonia Greteman

966

967

968

969

970

971

972

973

**966:** COMPANY: Old Hat Creative / CLIENT: Culver-Stockon College, Canton, MO / DESIGNER: Kris Bazen / ART DIRECTOR: Kris Bazen
**967:** COMPANY: leightonhubbell.com / CLIENT: San Jacinto College / DESIGNER: Leighton Hubbell / ART DIRECTOR: Leighton Hubbell
**968:** COMPANY: J Sayles Design Co. / CLIENT: Scornovaccas / DESIGNER: John Sayles / ART DIRECTOR: John Sayles
**969:** COMPANY: J Sayles Design Co. / CLIENT: Panteleakis Family / DESIGNER: John Sayles / ART DIRECTOR: John Sayles
**970:** COMPANY: Gyula Németh / DESIGNER: Gyula Németh
**971:** COMPANY: J Sayles Design Co. / CLIENT: Boy Scouts of Iowa / DESIGNER: John Sayles / ART DIRECTOR: John Sayles
**972:** COMPANY: Roy Smith Design / CLIENT: Lighting manufacturer / DESIGNER: Roy Smith
**973:** COMPANY: leightonhubbell.com / CLIENT: Heritage Palmcats / DESIGNER: Leighton Hubbell / ART DIRECTOR: Leighton Hubbell

975

974

976

WE MEAN CLEAN.

977

978

KLAUSMEYER
*Natural Medicine*

979

980

**974:** COMPANY: Banowetz & Company / CLIENT: White Rock Lake Conservancy / DESIGNER: Kris Murphy / ART DIRECTOR: Eric Venegas
**975:** COMPANY: Art Chantry Design / CLIENT: Joe Schwab, Euclid Records / DESIGNER: Art Chantry / ART DIRECTOR: Art Chantry
**976:** COMPANY: Derek Yoder / CLIENT: Rex's Rods & Customs / DESIGNER: Derek Yoder / ART DIRECTOR: Derek Yoder
**977:** COMPANY: Banowetz & Company / CLIENT: Pro Soap / DESIGNER: Sarah Terrell / ART DIRECTOR: Eric Venegas
**978:** COMPANY: Derek Yoder / CLIENT: Athletics / DESIGNER: Derek Yoder / ART DIRECTOR: Derek Yoder
**979:** COMPANY: Brent Couchman Design / CLIENT: Fossil / DESIGNER: Brent Couchman / ART DIRECTOR: Dru McCabe
**980:** COMPANY: Greteman Group / CLIENT: Klausmeyer Natural Medicine / DESIGNER: Chris Parks / ART DIRECTOR: Sonia Greteman

# NIKITA

**981**

**982**

Altitude

**983**

**984**

HEALTHY
Workplace Alliance
Advancing Employee Wellness

**985**

**986**

**981:** COMPANY: Chase Design Group / CLIENT: The CW / DESIGNERS: Jon Ariazza, Clark Goolsby / ART DIRECTOR: Margo Chase
**982:** COMPANY: Chris Rooney Illustration/Design / CLIENT: Silverpop / DESIGNER: Chris Rooney / ART DIRECTORS: Ken Cook, Brandtank
**983:** COMPANY: Gardner Design / CLIENT: Stonebridge Deli / DESIGNER: Brian Miller / ART DIRECTOR: Brian Miller
**984:** COMPANY: Greteman Group / CLIENT: Greteman Group / DESIGNER: Chris Parks / ART DIRECTOR: Sonia Greteman
**985:** COMPANY: Gardner Design / CLIENT: Charter Reserve / DESIGNER: Brian Miller / ART DIRECTOR: Brian Miller
**986:** COMPANY: Greteman Group / CLIENT: Royal Caribbean / DESIGNER: Chris Parks / ART DIRECTOR: Sonia Greteman

987

988

989

990

991

992

993

994

**987:** COMPANY: Michael Doret Graphic Design / CLIENT: Alphabet Soup / DESIGNER: Michael Doret / ART DIRECTOR: Michael Doret
**988:** COMPANY: Pollard Design / DESIGNER: Jeff Pollard
**989:** COMPANY: Pollard Design / DESIGNER: Jeff Pollard
**990:** COMPANY: Michael Doret Graphic Design / CLIENT: The Splinter Group / DESIGNER: Michael Doret / ART DIRECTOR: Lane Wurster
**991:** COMPANY: Michael Doret Graphic Design / CLIENT: Acme Studios / DESIGNER: Michael Doret / ART DIRECTOR: Adrian Olabuenaga
**992:** COMPANY: Jeremy Slagle Graphic Design / CLIENT: Pinchflat Bicycle Poster Show / DESIGNER: Jeremy Slagle / ART DIRECTOR: Jeremy Slagle
**993:** COMPANY: Pollard Design / DESIGNER: Jeff Pollard
**994:** COMPANY: Device / CLIENT: Archaia / DESIGNER: Rian Hughes / ART DIRECTOR: Rian Hughes

995

996

997

998

**MODERN FIBER**™
CARPET CLEANING

999

1000

1001

1002

995: COMPANY: Thrillustrate
996: COMPANY: Pollard Design / DESIGNER: Jeff Pollard
997: COMPANY: The Joe Bosack Graphic Design Co. / CLIENT: / DESIGNER: Joe Bosack / ART DIRECTOR: Joe Bosack
998: COMPANY: Invisible Creature / CLIENT: Invisible Creature / DESIGNER: Don Clark / ART DIRECTOR: Don Clark
999: COMPANY: Gravitate Design Studio / DESIGNER: Marc Neidlinger / ART DIRECTOR: Marc Neidlinger
1000: COMPANY: Sean Heisler / CLIENT: Schu-Shine Inn / DESIGNER: Sean Heisler / ART DIRECTOR: Sean Heisler
1001: COMPANY: Roy Smith Design / CLIENT: Josh Jaggard / DESIGNER: Roy Smith
1002: COMPANY: Mirko Ilic Corp. / CLIENT: Bachic Fine Jewelry / DESIGNER: Mirko Ilic / ART DIRECTOR: Mirko Ilic

# A Closer Look

**FIRM:** RANDY HEIL
**DESIGNER / ILLUSTRATOR:** RANDY HEIL
**ART DIRECTOR:** RANDY HEIL
**WRITER:** ZACH BROCKHOUSE
**CLIENT:** RANDY HEIL / R&R PARTNERS

How do you relieve the sting of disappointment when clients repeatedly choose the throwaway logo concept instead of the potential award-winning favorite? Become the client. Then throw a party.

The mustache party was a way for R&R Partners to celebrate facial hair and a way for me to create some work that would look great in my portfolio. I teamed up with brilliant copywriter Zach Brockhouse to design materials to promote the party. This included a logo to be used on posters, in email blasts, and on mirror clings.

Zach wrote some great headlines and copy for the posters and even volunteered to host the after–party where a trophy was awarded for the most outstanding mustache. I sported a Brimley and would have won, if not for corrupt judging and backroom politics. The party was a huge success and my wife told me I had a great time.

My work process differs from most, in that I design logos using my mouth. An auto accident in 1985 left me paralyzed and unable to use my legs and hands. I sketch with a pencil in my mouth and operate my Mac with a mouth-stick and Kensington trackball. I use the Mac OSX Sticky Keys feature and keyboard shortcuts whenever possible. When I need to sketch, I use an oversized sketchbook attached to an easel that mounts to the desktop. My thumbnail sketches can look a bit messy so I often forego thumbnails and concept directly in Adobe Illustrator.

I feel fortunate that my work can inspire others. I'm also thankful to work for an agency that recognizes my abilities rather than my disabilities.

*This mark falls outside the standard tightly knit logo work we've come to expect from Heil. It's loose, rough, monochromatic, yet perfect. If I didn't know any better, I'd say he tore it from the back of an antique sarsaparilla bottle.*

*The unmistakable personality of this logo sets the perfect tone for their company party and contest, and it shows contestants the proper 'stache size to shoot for if you want to compete.*

The accompanying posters that donned the logo are clever interactive pieces allowing the viewer to slide, select, and study potential styles to grow and groom.

If the posters weren't enough, Heil provided mirror clings of many of the mustache styles, so contestants could "test drive" these beauties before their stubble began to fill in.

1003

1004

1006

1005

1007

1008

1009

**1003:** COMPANY: Schwartzrock Graphic Arts / CLIENT: BI Worldwide / DESIGNER: Sherwin Schwartzrock
**1004:** COMPANY: Schwartzrock Graphic Arts / CLIENT: Community Comics / DESIGNER: Sherwin Schwartzrock
**1005:** COMPANY: Schwartzrock Graphic Arts / CLIENT: BI Worldwide / DESIGNER: Sherwin Schwartzrock
**1006:** COMPANY: J. Sayles Design Co. / CLIENT: Animal Rescue League of Iowa / DESIGNER: John Sayles / ART DIRECTOR: John Sayles
**1007:** COMPANY: Karen Holum Design / CLIENT: Kowalgo Holding Co. / DESIGNER: Art Chantry / ART DIRECTOR: Art Chantry
**1008:** COMPANY: Voov Ltd. / CLIENT: Ginapron Ltd. / DESIGNER: Bálint Egyed / ART DIRECTOR: Bálint Egyed
**1009:** COMPANY: Schwartzrock Graphic Arts / CLIENT: Target / DESIGNER: Sherwin Schwartzrock

1010

1011

1012

1013

momentus™

1014

1015

Hampster

1016

1010: COMPANY: H2 Design of Texas / CLIENT: King Shake / DESIGNER: Hoyt Haffelder / ART DIRECTOR: Hoyt Haffelder
1011: COMPANY: Star Group / CLIENT: AMNRL / DESIGNER: Scott Oeschger / ART DIRECTOR: Scott Oeschger
1012: CLIENT: Harlow's Donuts / DESIGNER: Kyle Dingman
1013: COMPANY: Design Center, Inc. / CLIENT: CIS / DESIGNER: Sherwin Schwartzrock
1014: COMPANY: Chase Design Group / CLIENT: ecoAmerica / DESIGNERS: Paula Hansanugrum, Evangeline Joo / ART DIRECTORS: Margo Chase, Paula Hansanugrum
1015: COMPANY: Schwartzrock Graphic Arts / CLIENT: BI Worldwide / DESIGNER: Sherwin Schwartzrock
1016: COMPANY: R&R Partners / CLIENT: Hampton Roads Transit / DESIGNER: Randy Heil / ART DIRECTOR: Randy Heil

1017

1018

1019

1020

1021

1022

1023

1024

**1017:** COMPANY: Art Chantry Design / CLIENT: Ride Snow Boards / DESIGNER: Art Chantry / ART DIRECTOR: Art Chantry
**1018:** COMPANY: atomicvibe / CLIENT: Steep This! / DESIGNER: Jon Stapp / ART DIRECTOR: Jon Stapp
**1019:** COMPANY: Darwin Avenue / CLIENT: Eclectic Monkey Emporium / DESIGNER: Jason Johnson / ART DIRECTOR: Jason Johnson
**1020:** COMPANY: Greteman Group / CLIENT: Chris Brunner / DESIGNER: Sonia Greteman / ART DIRECTOR: Sonia Greteman
**1021:** COMPANY: Gardner Design / CLIENT: Bluebird Books / DESIGNER: Brian Miller / ART DIRECTOR: Brian Miller
**1022:** COMPANY: Gardner Design / CLIENT: Pauline Reese / DESIGNER: Brian Miller / ART DIRECTOR: Brian Miller
**1023:** COMPANY: Gardner Design / CLIENT: Mystik Butterfly / DESIGNER: Brian Miller / ART DIRECTOR: Brian Miller
**1024:** COMPANY: Greteman Group / CLIENT: City of Derby / DESIGNER: Garrett Fresh / ART DIRECTOR: Sonia Greteman

1025

FINAL FRIDAY

1026

1027

THE TRAINS AT NORTHPARK

**Benefiting**
**Ronald McDonald House of Dallas**

1028

BRICK ST PIZZA

1029

1030

BOTANICA
WICHITA

1031

VENTUS
Custom Cycles

1032

1025: COMPANY: WORKtoDATE (www.worktodate.com) / CLIENT: WORKtoDATE / DESIGNER: Greg Bennett / ART DIRECTOR: Greg Bennett
1026: COMPANY: Greteman Group / CLIENT: Wichita Economic Development / DESIGNER: Garrett Fresh / ART DIRECTOR: Sonia Greteman
1027: COMPANY: Chris Rooney Illustration/Design / CLIENT: Workout Bus / DESIGNER: Chris Rooney
1028: COMPANY: Banowetz & Company / CLIENT: The Trains at NorthPark / DESIGNER: Eric Venegas / ART DIRECTOR: Eric Venegas
1029: COMPANY: Base Art Co. / CLIENT: Donatos Pizza / DESIGNER: Drue Dixon / ART DIRECTOR: Terry Rohrback
1030: COMPANY: Gyula Németh / DESIGNER: Gyula Németh
1031: COMPANY: Greteman Group / CLIENT: Botanica Gardens / DESIGNER: Chris Parks / ART DIRECTOR: Sonia Greteman
1032: COMPANY: Adam Anderson / DESIGNER: Adam Anderson

1033

1034

1035

1036

1037

1038

1039

# playc●re

**1040**

**1041**

**1042**

**1044**

**1043**

**1045**

**1040:** COMPANY: Jon Flaming Design / CLIENT: PlayCore / DESIGNER: Jon Flaming / ART DIRECTOR: Jon Flaming
**1041:** COMPANY: Baji Group / CLIENT: Pedal Craft / DESIGNER: Jonny Ashcroft
**1042:** COMPANY: J Sayles Design Co. / CLIENT: Beth El Jacob / Synagogue / DESIGNER: John Sayles / ART DIRECTOR: John Sayles
**1043:** COMPANY: The Joe Bosack Graphic Design Co. / DESIGNER: Joe Bosack / ART DIRECTOR: Joe Bosack
**1044:** COMPANY: Bailey Lauerman / CLIENT: Bailey Lauerman / DESIGNER: Brandon Oitman / ART DIRECTOR: Carter Weitz
**1045:** CLIENT: Hana Lena / DESIGNER: Jude Landry

1046

1047

1048

1049

1050

1051

1052

1053

**1046:** COMPANY: leightonhubbell.com / CLIENT: San Jacinto College / DESIGNER: Leighton Hubbell / ART DIRECTOR: Leighton Hubbell
**1047:** COMPANY: Jeremy Slagle Graphic Design / CLIENT: Teodora's Kitchen / DESIGNER: Jeremy Slagle / ART DIRECTOR: Jeremy Slagle
**1048:** COMPANY: leightonhubbell.com / CLIENT: Tiddlywinks Toys and Games / DESIGNER: Leighton Hubbell / ART DIRECTOR: Leighton Hubbell
**1049:** COMPANY: Sean Heisler / CLIENT: Tatuana Trading Company / DESIGNER: Sean Heisler / ART DIRECTOR: Sean Heisler
**1050:** COMPANY: Pollard Design / DESIGNER: Jeff Pollard
**1051:** COMPANY: a: design / CLIENT: Victor Miranda / DESIGNER: Ana Paula Rodrigues / ART DIRECTOR: Ana Paula Rodrigues
**1052:** COMPANY: Pollard Design / DESIGNER: Jeff Pollard
**1053:** COMPANY: REACTOR design Studio / CLIENT: Arts Council of Johnson County / DESIGNER: Chase Wilson / ART DIRECTOR: Clifton Alexander

1054

1055

1056

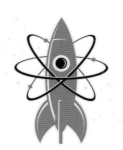

1057

1058

1059

1060

1061

**1054:** COMPANY: Thrillustrate
**1055:** COMPANY: RDG Advertising / CLIENT: Casino/ Gaming Special Events / DESIGNER: Shane Cawthon / ART DIRECTOR: Angelo Ramirez
**1056:** COMPANY: Throttle Design Mechanics / CLIENT: Pharaohs Street Rodders / DESIGNER: John Nissen / ART DIRECTOR: Dave Adamson
**1057:** COMPANY: Timber Design Co. / DESIGNER: Lars Lawson
**1058:** COMPANY: Mattson Creative / DESIGNER: Ty Mattson
**1059:** COMPANY: Weather Control / CLIENT: Eddie Bauer / DESIGNER: Josh Oakley
**1060:** COMPANY: Articulate Solutions / CLIENT: Monterey Bay Services / DESIGNER: Clint G. Delapaz / ART DIRECTOR: Katherine L Filice
**1061:** COMPANY: Weather Control / CLIENT: Sasquatch Music Festival / DESIGNER: Josh Oakley

**FIRM:** DEVICE
**DESIGNER / ILLUSTRATOR:** RIAN HUGHES
**ART DIRECTOR:** KEN LOPEZ
**CLIENT:** DC COMICS

It has been a pleasure to work with DC comics on various projects through the years. Each one brings its own unique set of challenges and results. I have been commissioned to design two Batgirl logos in my time working with them (prior to "The New 52" reboot). I was pleased with how my first redesign came out, but with the second, the project took a completely unexpected turn. I gave DC many directions to choose from initially, but they felt that they were all too whimsical, feminine, and bouncy. They noted that they were looking for a good balance between retro and modern because of the seriousness of the book series. DC gave me a look at the new Batgirl costume for additional reference and decided that it was best to explore more simple and modern shapes for the bat with possibly a couple more literal versions thrown in.

In the end, the client chose a redesign that was a complete departure from the initial redesign that I did. To finalize the chosen logo I added additional cuts in the chunky letters and detail in the bat shape to make it feel less juvenile. The logo sold through and worked well across the top of the comics, but I hope someday that we can revisit the possibility of DC adopting one of the other directions that was a bit more classic and feminine.

*These two Batgirl logo reboots (above; top two, opposite) each evoke completely different reactions from viewers. The first redesign for Cassandra Cain as Batgirl, combines a nontypical asymmetry with a slightly playful femininity in the eyes and overall batwing shape. The bold, masculine type brings a solid heroic feel to the final mark. This logo is bold enough to be stenciled in spraypaint, yet sexy enough to be envied by Wonder Woman. The Yvonne Craig—era purple-and-gold color palette is a perfect fit for this logo's slightly mod '60s freestyle feel.*

*I can image that DC loved seeing all these tight explorations enroute to the final design. The custom-type treatments combined with feminine batwing variations are diverse, flirty, and engaging. Choosing appropriate design cues from this set to incorporate into a final logo must have been difficult—they are all so stellar.*

*The second batgirl reboot logo is much more traditional in its approach to the batwing treatment. The custom type is decidedly more static, but still has some subtle dimensionality involved.*

*This study of positive and negative space is brilliant. The logo across Batgirl's bare chest makes you wonder if she even needs a logo sewn into her costume.*

*The logo displayed here plays upon the same dimensionality seen in the caped logo designs of the mid '60s. Along with the blue highlights, the mark is a more 3-D evolution of Hughes' first reboot logo. Personally, this logo could be my favorite superhero logo in the history of comics. Too bad it was never utilized.*

**RESCUE**

1062

1063

1064

1065

Architectural Real Estate

EnVISAGE

1066

lucid

1067

1068

**1062:** COMPANY: R&R Partners / CLIENT: Rescue / DESIGNER: Randy Heil / ART DIRECTOR: Randy Heil
**1063:** COMPANY: Schwartzrock Graphic Arts / CLIENT: I. V. Desk / DESIGNER: Sherwin Schwartzrock
**1064:** COMPANY: 5Seven / CLIENT: UTAP Printing / DESIGNER: Clint G. Delapaz / ART DIRECTOR: Clint G. Delapaz
**1065:** COMPANY: Schwartzrock Graphic Arts / CLIENT: Charpentier Hovland Advertising / DESIGNER: Sherwin Schwartzrock
**1066:** COMPANY: Schwartzrock Graphic Arts / CLIENT: Derek Dertus / DESIGNER: Sherwin Schwartzrock
**1067:** COMPANY: Schwartzrock Graphic Arts / CLIENT: Lucid Labs / DESIGNER: Sherwin Schwartzrock
**1068:** COMPANY: Design Center, Inc. / CLIENT: Franciscan Health / DESIGNER: Sherwin Schwartzrock / ART DIRECTOR: John Reger

1069

TRADE MARK
ecommerce
MECHANICS

1070

1071

*Control Your Cash*

1072

COMMUNITY CHRISTIAN SCHOOL

1073

1074

1075

**1069:** COMPANY: Schwartzrock Graphic Arts / CLIENT: 3.2.1. Inc. / DESIGNER: Sherwin Schwartzrock
**1070:** COMPANY: Schwartzrock Graphic Arts / CLIENT: Brad Radtke / DESIGNER: Sherwin Schwartzrock
**1071:** COMPANY: Schwartzrock Graphic Arts / CLIENT: Kingstone Media / DESIGNER: Sherwin Schwartzrock
**1072:** COMPANY: R&R Partners / CLIENT: Control Your Cash / DESIGNER: Randy Heil / ART DIRECTOR: Randy Heil
**1073:** COMPANY: Schwartzrock Graphic Arts / CLIENT: Community Christian School / DESIGNER: Sherwin Schwartzrock
**1074:** DESIGNER: Floris Voorveld / ART DIRECTOR: Floris Voorveld
**1075:** COMPANY: Robert Finkel Design / CLIENT: BeeHouse / DESIGNER: Robert Finkel / ART DIRECTOR: Robert Finkel

1076

1077

1078

1079

1080

1081

1082

1083

**1076:** COMPANY: Schwartzrock Graphic Arts / CLIENT: Brad Radtke and Associates / DESIGNER: Sherwin Schwartzrock
**1077:** COMPANY: Flight Deck Creative / CLIENT: James Hogue / DESIGNER: Jason Rahn / ART DIRECTOR: Jason Rahn
**1078:** COMPANY: Gyula Németh / DESIGNER: Gyula Németh
**1079:** COMPANY: Flight Deck Creative / CLIENT: Tom Grothouse / DESIGNER: Jason Rahn / ART DIRECTOR: Jason Rahn
**1080:** COMPANY: The Joe Bosack Graphic Design Co. / DESIGNER: Joe Bosack / ART DIRECTOR: Joe Bosack
**1081:** COMPANY: Gyula Németh / DESIGNER: Gyula Németh
**1082:** COMPANY: leightonhubbell.com / CLIENT: Leisure Interactive / DESIGNER: Leighton Hubbell / ART DIRECTOR: Leighton Hubbell
**1083:** COMPANY: J Sayles Design Co. / CLIENT: Tifereth / DESIGNER: John Sayles / ART DIRECTOR: John Sayles

grow in style

1084

LIC# 965478

1085

1086

1087

NEW CITY CHURCH

1088

1089

1090

1091

**1084:** COMPANY: Mode Design / CLIENT: Moss Style Hair Salon / DESIGNER: Hans Bennewitz / ART DIRECTOR: Hans Bennewitz
**1085:** COMPANY: Mode Design / CLIENT: Brett Drury / DESIGNER: Hans Bennewitz / ART DIRECTOR: Hans Bennewitz
**1086:** COMPANY: Gyula Németh / DESIGNER: Gyula Németh
**1087:** COMPANY: Gyula Németh / DESIGNER: Gyula Németh
**1088:** COMPANY: Baji Group / CLIENT: New City Church / DESIGNER: Jonny Ashcroft
**1089:** COMPANY: J Sayles Design Co. / CLIENT: New York City Pizza / DESIGNER: John Sayles / ART DIRECTOR: John Sayles
**1090:** COMPANY: Jon Flaming Design / CLIENT: Urbana Communities / DESIGNER: Jon Flaming / ART DIRECTOR: Jon Flaming
**1091:** COMPANY: Gyula Németh / DESIGNER: Gyula Németh

1092

1093

1094

1095

1096

CAYMANN
ENTERTAINMENT

1097

1098

1092: COMPANY: REACTOR design Studio / CLIENT: Freelancers University / DESIGNER: Chase Wilson / ART DIRECTOR: Clifton Alexander
1093: COMPANY: Chase Design Group / CLIENT: Mattel Game / DESIGNERS: Ritzelle Cayabyab, Evangeline Joo / ART DIRECTOR: Margo Chase
1094: COMPANY: Jeremy Slagle Graphic Desogn / CLIENT: Quaint Co. / DESIGNER: Jeremy Slagle / ART DIRECTOR: Jeremy Slagle
1095: COMPANY: Michael Doret Graphic Design / CLIENT: Rod Dyer International / DESIGNER: Michael Doret / ART DIRECTOR: Rod Dyer
1096: CLIENT: Vitaliy Vorona / DESIGNER: Artem Dvorzhak
1097: COMPANY: Sean Heisler / CLIENT: Caymann Entertainment / DESIGNER: Sean Heisler / ART DIRECTOR: Sean Heisler
1098: COMPANY: leightonhubbell.com / CLIENT: Tiddlywinks Toys and Games / DESIGNER: Leighton Hubbell / ART DIRECTOR: Leighton Hubbell

# Confluence Unlimited

1099

1100

Grizedale
Lodge

1101

1102

**SQUASH BC**

1103

1104

**1099:** COMPANY: Jeremy Slagle Graphic Design / CLIENT: Confluence Unlimited / DESIGNER: Jeremy Slagle / ART DIRECTOR: Jeremy Slagle
**1100:** COMPANY: Pollard Design / DESIGNER: Jeff Pollard
**1101:** COMPANY: Roy Smith Design / CLIENT: Grizedale Lodge / DESIGNER: Roy Smith
**1102:** COMPANY: Salvadore Anguiano / CLIENT: Vato Clothing / DESIGNER: Salvadore Anguiano / ART DIRECTOR: Salvadore Anguiano
**1103:** COMPANY: Pacey + Pacey Design / CLIENT: Squash BC / DESIGNER: Robert Pacey / ART DIRECTOR: Michael Pacey
**1104:** COMPANY: Pollard Design / DESIGNER: Jeff Pollard

1105

1106

1107

1108

1109

1110

1111

1112

1105: COMPANY: Throttle Design Mechanics / CLIENT: Les Schwab Tires / DESIGNER: Wendel Hayes / ART DIRECTOR: Dave Adamson
1106: COMPANY: Schwartzrock Graphic Arts / CLIENT: Werner Design Werks / DESIGNER: Sherwin Schwartzrock
1107: COMPANY: Schwartzrock Graphic Arts / CLIENT: American Bible Society / DESIGNER: Sherwin Schwartzrock
1108: COMPANY: Schwartzrock Graphic Arts / CLIENT: Christy / DESIGNER: Sherwin Schwartzrock
1109: COMPANY: Invisible Creature / CLIENT: Invisible Creature / DESIGNER: Don Clark / ART DIRECTOR: Don Clark
1110: COMPANY: R&R Partners / CLIENT: Honolulu Rail Transit / DESIGNER: Randy Heil / ART DIRECTOR: Randy Heil
1111: COMPANY: Invisible Creature / CLIENT: Tour Machine / DESIGNER: Ryan Clark / ART DIRECTOR: Ryan Clark
1112: COMPANY: R&R Partners / CLIENT: R&R Partners / DESIGNER: Randy Heil / ART DIRECTOR: Randy Heil

1113

1114

CAPELLA
TOWER

1115

1116

1117

1118

1119

1113: COMPANY: Schwartzrock Graphic Arts / CLIENT: Franke + Fiorella / DESIGNER: Sherwin Schwartzrock
1114: COMPANY: ACTUART LP / CLIENT: girlstalkinsmack.com / DESIGNER: Peter Vasvari / ART DIRECTOR: Peter Vasvari
1115: COMPANY: Sussner Design Company / CLIENT: Ryan Companies / DESIGNER: Danielle Dressner / ART DIRECTOR: Derek Sussner
1116: COMPANY: Schwartzrock Graphic Arts / CLIENT: DSFederal / DESIGNER: Sherwin Schwartzrock
1117: COMPANY: Ramp / CLIENT: Santangiolina / DESIGNER: Oliver Lan, Kristen Williams / ART DIRECTOR: Michael Stinson
1118: COMPANY: Nissen Design / CLIENT: Middle School Youth Group / DESIGNER: John Nissen / ART DIRECTOR: John Nissen
1119: COMPANY: Star Group / CLIENT: AMNRL / DESIGNER: Scott Oeschger / ART DIRECTOR: Scott Oeschger

**DESIGNER / ILLUSTRATOR:** FELIX SOCKWELL
**CREATIVE STRATEGIST:** GUTHRIE DOLAN
**CLIENT:** ODOPOD

A while back, Odopod called and had me do some ideation for Zynga, the leader in gaming design. At the time I was working on the front, log-in page for Facebook, which is a partner with Zynga.

Initially, I chose to use the existing mark because it reduces well and has brand equity as an excuse to allow for a leash that wakes up the dog when it's time to play. Then we went broader, to a circus—the big tent. As I look back on the exploration, it's funny. I only had two or three days to work so I jumped in and started right away, not realizing I had spelled the name of the company wrong! (Zynga is with a *y* not an *i*). The rest of the ideas are various iterations of the company owner's dog Zynga in various forms; with a trophy, as a line (to show connections) and so forth.

In the end, the agency (and client) did the right thing; nothing. The existing Zynga silhouette could not be improved to an extent worthy of an identity overhaul. When I see it now as I play Words with Friends (owned by Zynga) I have to say it reduces well and does its job.

*Many gamers are attracted to gaming for the achievements, leveling up, and awards they win along the way. Sockwell speaks to this successfully by incorporating the trophy icon into the logo to resemble the letter Y. The added equity of the existing bulldog interacting with it in various ways brings it all home. (opposite page, top)*

*This circus tent entrance feels like the best solution for this project. It's graphic, contemporary, and communicates well. The tent graphic invites you into Zynga's arcade and makes you feel like you could immerse yourself in a boundless alternate universe of gaming forever.*

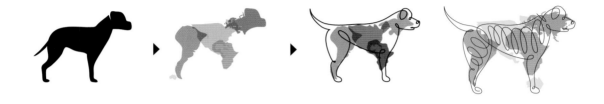

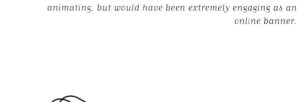

*I enjoy imagining the animation potential of this progression of a leash evolving into the logotype and then tugging at the dog, encouraging him to play. This would have taken some precise animating, but would have been extremely engaging as an online banner.*

*These explorations are reminiscent of the decorative drop caps you'd find in children's books or illuminated manuscripts. They are very playful and have a hand-rendered look and feel. If court jesters from the middle ages had uniforms, I could see these logos being embroidered onto the left chests.*

1120

# CHAPADA

*Chophouse and Churrascaria*

1121

1122

1123

1124

# GENT ORGANIC MUSTACHE WAX

1125

SCENE ON MAIN
URBAN. COCKTAILS. CUISINE.

1126

**1120:** COMPANY: Adam Anderson / DESIGNER: Adam Anderson
**1121:** COMPANY: Gardner Design / CLIENT: Chapada Chophouse and Churrascaria / DESIGNER: Brian Miller / ART DIRECTOR: Brian Miller
**1122:** COMPANY: Chase Design Group / CLIENT: Califia Farms / DESIGNER: Margo Chase, Paula Hansanugrum / ART DIRECTOR: Margo Chase
**1123:** COMPANY: Banowetz & Company / CLIENT: El Fenix Tex-Mex Express / DESIGNER: Eric Venegas / ART DIRECTOR: Eric Venegas
**1124:** COMPANY: atomicvibe / CLIENT: Sweet Toof Bakery / DESIGNER: Jon Stapp / ART DIRECTOR: Jon Stapp
**1125:** COMPANY: Adam Anderson / DESIGNER: Adam Anderson
**1126:** COMPANY: Banowetz & Company / CLIENT: Scene on Main / DESIGNER: Kris Murphy / ART DIRECTOR: Eric Venegas

PLAYERS
SPORT CLUB
AT TREETOPS

1127

1128

1129

KETCH

1130

the Vampire Diaries

1131

DULCE MÉXICO™

1132

1133

1127: COMPANY: Schwartzrock Graphic Arts / CLIENT: RiverBrand Design / DESIGNER: Sherwin Schwartzrock
1128: COMPANY: Gardner Design / CLIENT: Bradley Paper / DESIGNER: Brian Miller / ART DIRECTOR: Brian Miller
1129: COMPANY: Chase Design Group / CLIENT: LAAC - IAC Aerobatic Chapter / DESIGNER: Margo Chase / ART DIRECTOR: Margo Chase
1130: COMPANY: Gardner Design / CLIENT: KETCH / DESIGNER: Adam Anderson / ART DIRECTOR: Brian Miller
1131: COMPANY: Chase Design Group / CLIENT: The CW / DESIGNER: Margo Chase / ART DIRECTOR: Margo Chase
1132: CLIENT: Dulce Mexico / DESIGNER: Robert Cho / ART DIRECTOR: Robert Cho
1133: COMPANY: Gardner Design / CLIENT: The Church of the Latter Day Saints / DESIGNER: Brian Miller / ART DIRECTOR: Brian Miller

1134

1135

1136

1137

1138

1139

1140

1141

**1134:** COMPANY: Gardner Design / CLIENT: Sand Creek Station / DESIGNER: Elisabeth Owens / ART DIRECTOR: Brian Miller
**1135:** COMPANY: The Joe Bosack Graphic Design Co. / DESIGNER: Joe Bosack / ART DIRECTOR: Joe Bosack
**1136:** COMPANY: Greteman Group / CLIENT: Horses to Humans / DESIGNER: Garrett Fresh / ART DIRECTOR: Sonia Greteman
**1137:** COMPANY: Logo Planet Laboratory / CLIENT: Bagel'd / DESIGNER: Jeffrey Mardis
**1138:** COMPANY: J Sayles Design Co. / CLIENT: J Sayles Design Co. / DESIGNER: John Sayles / ART DIRECTOR: John Sayles
**1139:** COMPANY: Hatch Design / CLIENT: Wine Luxury / DESIGNER: Jeffrey Bucholtz / ART DIRECTORS: Joel Templin, Katie Jain
**1140:** COMPANY: 26am / CLIENT: 7 Sirens Rum / DESIGNER: Hans Bennewitz / ART DIRECTOR: David Sudarma
**1141:** COMPANY: Hatch Design / CLIENT: Khol's / DESIGNER: Eszter Clark / ART DIRECTORS: Joel Templin, Katie Jain

1142

1143

1144

RALPH SMYTH
ENTERTAINMENT

1145

1146

1147

WHITE OAK
AMPHITHEATRE

1148

1149

**1142:** COMPANY: The Joe Bosack Graphic Design Co. / DESIGNER: Joe Bosack / ART DIRECTOR: Joe Bosack
**1143:** COMPANY: leightonhubbell.com / DESIGNER: Leighton Hubbell / ART DIRECTOR: Leighton Hubbell
**1144:** COMPANY: Gyula Németh / DESIGNER: Gyula Németh
**1145:** COMPANY: Joseph Blalock Design Office / CLIENT: Ralph Smyth Entertainment / DESIGNER: Joseph Blalock
**1146:** COMPANY: Kris Bazen Creative / CLIENT: Middlesex Islanders Hockey Club, Tyngsboro, MA / DESIGNER: Kris Bazen / ART DIRECTOR: Kris Bazen
**1147:** COMPANY: leightonhubbell.com / CLIENT: Leisure Interactive / DESIGNER: Leighton Hubbell / ART DIRECTOR: Leighton Hubbell
**1148:** COMPANY: The Joe Bosack Graphic Design Co. / DESIGNER: Joe Bosack / ART DIRECTOR: Joe Bosack
**1149:** COMPANY: leightonhubbell.com / CLIENT: Outrageous California BBQ / DESIGNER: Leighton Hubbell / ART DIRECTOR: Leighton Hubbell

ONEY

ROOFING COMPANY

1150

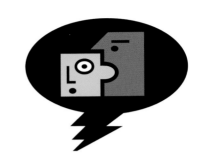

1151

GRANDIUS SLAMMUS

1152

SCOTCH PLAINS
PUBLIC LIBRARY

IN THE TIME OF THE

Butterflies

1153

NEW YORK
STATE
RESTAURANT
ASSOCIATION

1154

Riverside
ANIMAL CARE

1155

curlysheep

1156

**1150:** COMPANY: leightonhubbell.com / CLIENT: Oney Roofing / DESIGNER: Leighton Hubbell / ART DIRECTOR: Leighton Hubbell
**1151:** COMPANY: Pollard Design / DESIGNER: Jeff Pollard
**1152:** COMPANY: Pollard Design / DESIGNER: Jeff Pollard
**1153:** COMPANY: a: design / CLIENT: Scotch Plains Public Library (New Jersey) / DESIGNER: Ana Paula Rodrigues / ART DIRECTOR: Ana Paula Rodrigues
**1154:** COMPANY: C&G Partners / CLIENT: New York State Restaurant Association / DESIGNER: Hyun Auh / ART DIRECTOR: Steff Geissbuhler
**1155:** COMPANY: Jeremy Slagle Graphic Design / CLIENT: Riverside Animal Care / DESIGNER: Jeremy Slagle / ART DIRECTOR: Jeremy Slagle
**1156:** COMPANY: Atom Design / CLIENT: Curly Sheep. Eco-Ethno Manufactories / DESIGNER: Lana Gruic (Vitas) / ART DIRECTOR: Lana Gruic (Vitas)

# BUDWEISER

**1157**

**1158**

**1159**

**1160**

AROMAS
• POSTRES Y DULCES •

**1161**

**1162**

1157: COMPANY: Jamie Sheehan Design / CLIENT: Anhauser Busch Brewery / DESIGNER: Art Chantry / ART DIRECTOR: Jamie Sheehan
1158: COMPANY: Mattson Creative / DESIGNER: Ty Mattson
1159: COMPANY: Invisible Creature / CLIENT: Superhero Artist Management / DESIGNER: Ryan Clark / ART DIRECTOR: Ryan Clark
1160: COMPANY: Salvadore Anguiano / CLIENT: Aromas Restaurant / DESIGNER: Salvadore Anguiano / ART DIRECTOR: Salvadore Anguiano
1161: COMPANY: Salvadore Anguiano / CLIENT: Bimotec / DESIGNER: Salvadore Anguiano / ART DIRECTOR: Salvadore Anguiano
1162: COMPANY: Mint / CLIENT: Mint / DESIGNER: Mike Calkins

**VOCABRA**

1163

code burger

1164

1165

1166

1167

1168

1169

1170

**1163:** COMPANY: Schwartzrock Graphic Arts / CLIENT: Vocabra / DESIGNER: Sherwin Schwartzrock
**1164:** COMPANY: Jared Granger / CLIENT: Exploration / DESIGNER: Jared Granger / ART DIRECTOR: Jared Granger
**1165:** COMPANY: Fairchild Creative / CLIENT: MAKO Cement Screeds / DESIGNER: Douglas Fairchild / ART DIRECTOR: Douglas Fairchild
**1166:** COMPANY: Atom Design / CLIENT: Glazzed, Fashion Accessories / DESIGNER: Lana Gruic (Vitas) / ART DIRECTOR: Lana Gruic (Vitas)
**1167:** COMPANY: Robert Finkel Design / CLIENT: Memphis Food Truckers Alliance / DESIGNER: Robert Finkel / ART DIRECTOR: Robert Finkel
**1168:** COMPANY: H2 Design of Texas / CLIENT: Outdoor Lighting Perspiective / DESIGNER: Hoyt Haffelder / ART DIRECTOR: Hoyt Haffelder
**1169:** COMPANY: Sussner Design Company / CLIENT: Linden Hills Co-op / DESIGNER: Brandon Van Lieve / ART DIRECTOR: Derek Sussner
**1170:** COMPANY: Invisible Creature / CLIENT: All American Rejects / DESIGNER: Ryan Clark / ART DIRECTOR: Ryan Clark

**BIRCHILL**
SCHOOL OF MOTORING

1171

THE **HOUSE** MODESTO

1172

1173

1174

1175

tiempo

1176

1177

1178

1171: COMPANY: Enrich Design / CLIENT: Birchill School of Motoring / DESIGNER: Kyle Richardson / ART DIRECTOR: Kyle Richardson
1172: COMPANY: Schwartzrock Graphic Arts / CLIENT: Worlds of Wow / DESIGNER: Sherwin Schwartzrock / ART DIRECTOR:
1173: COMPANY: Sussner Design Company / CLIENT: Sussner Design Company / DESIGNER: Ben Alpert / ART DIRECTOR: Derek Sussner
1174: COMPANY: Bailey Lauerman / CLIENT: Mid-Continent Technologies / DESIGNER: Brandon Oitman / ART DIRECTOR: Ron Sack, Carter Weitz
1175: COMPANY: Felix Sockwell / CLIENT: ENZACTA / DESIGNER: Felix Sockwell / ART DIRECTOR: David Brier
1176: COMPANY: Tactix Creative, Inc. / CLIENT: Tiempo Property Management / DESIGNER: Paul Howalt
1177: COMPANY: Tactix Creative, Inc. / CLIENT: Frost Orthodontics / DESIGNER: Paul Howalt
1178: COMPANY: Bailey Lauerman / CLIENT: AIGA Nebraska / DESIGNERS: Michael Schwab, Brandon Oitman, Jim Buhrman, Jr. / ART DIRECTOR: Ron Sack

# Design for a Nonprofit

JUSTIN AHRENS

*a*  *b*

## Investment and Expectation

At the beginning of my career, through a combination of wonderful events, I was able to meet rock legend Alice Cooper. It would be hard to find another musician that is as open to creative space as Alice is, so needless to say, I was pretty excited. Alice and a good friend of his started an organization called Solid Rock to provide kids in Phoenix with a safe place to hang out, study, learn about music and dance, and in general just feel secure. My partners and I thought this would be a great organization to support because we believed in its mission, and we felt it would be great PR. We used our entire network of writers, artists, photographers, and printers, to help this fledgling organization get off the ground. For the most part it was fun, but the work itself was challenging. We worked primarily on the core brand: fundraising events with elaborate themes. All of these projects typically started with the logo (fig. a, b) and basic brand development, which took us through several rounds of design and approval by committee. Some of it was exactly what we had hoped for, and other parts never made it to the level that we had planned. As the years went by, I found myself asking if we should continue doing this since the work wasn't as good as I knew it could be.

Everyone wanted the organization to be successful. We wanted to help with process, branding, communication, and we wanted to consistently raise the level and effectiveness of the mission and messaging. But each year it seemed to get harder instead of easier. It took me fifteen years to finally figure out that the issue was on both sides of the fence. Rule 29 loved Solid Rock and the people in it, and they loved us, but throughout the organization there wasn't the level of buy-in for what we were trying to achieve. And because we had invested so many years, we didn't want to let it go, so the work became frustrating.

We eventually ended our involvement with Solid Rock, and I mourned that separation. But time brings perspective, and I finally understood that this type of work is "not about you." I know this is hard to accept, because our ideas come from inside our hearts, brains, and souls. We can invest so much energy into something, knowing it has power, ROI, and impact—but if we lose sight of the mission and the reason for our initial involvement, we lose the ability to manage the project appropriately.

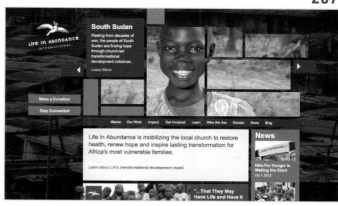

We remained one of Solid Rock's biggest fans, and I'm happy to say we have recently started working with them again after two years. The energy is back, and with it a fresh perspective on ways to communicate and a new understanding of everyone's roles and expectations.

**Trust and Collaboration**
In 2006 Rule 29 started doing work for an organization called Life in Abundance (LIA) International that helps the poor in some of the most challenging places in sub-Saharan Africa. From the very first project, I realized this was going to be a different type of relationship.

Like most of us, when we start a branding project we begin with the logo. In this case, the founder insisted the logo stay as it was. Having learned from Solid Rock, I knew I had to present the reasons why the logo needed to change while making sure the founder knew I was listening, understood the mission, and would keep as much of what she liked about the logo as I could. Additionally, I had to find a way to communicate that, as her new brand partner, the logo had to work for the organization in the United States, for European fundraising, and be seen as an acceptable mark in the variety of African countries LIA worked with. These would be new challenges for both LIA and Rule29.

The old blue bird logo—which I called the "war bird"—didn't communicate the help, peace, and friendliness it needed to. But knowing that we needed to keep a bird image, we explored the iconography for the main countries in Africa where the logo would appear, different colors, and other options. We read statistics and tried to wrap our heads around what those meant—and how it could really be that bad in so many areas. Through many conversations and a trip to Africa, a clearer picture of the need, the people, and the statistics emerged for me. We needed a bold logo, as well as one that was simple, peaceful, and hope-filled. After many iterations, I presented our solution to the founder, and I asked her to trust what we were doing because we "got" what she was doing (fig. c, d).

In the end, is creating a logo for a nonprofit different than creating a logo for any other company? In many ways, no. But in some incredible ways, definitely yes. Mission-driven or cause-related organizations demand a deep understanding and commitment on the part of the design firm, with awareness that the statistics that define the challenge and its impact are more than mere numbers—they are based on living things and real people. Work like this demands sensitivity, honesty, and dignity—these are crucial to the process.

**The Moral of the Stories**
Designing for a nonprofit is about so much more than donating your talent. There are inherent challenges and personal cost that can bring frustration—or unbelievable satisfaction and growth. The next time you are approached by a nonprofit, here are some things to keep in mind:

1. If you choose to do this work, sell out for it—believe in the mission or don't do it.

2. Be patient; communicate the process and its potential.

3. Listen.

4. Treat statistics with dignity.

5. Let the experience change you; serving tends to do that.

6. If you don't understand something, go experience it.

7. Find organizations you can mutually trust and collaborate with.

And above all, remember that you have the chance to help change the world … and that's just flat-out awesome.

1179

1180

1181

citychickie

1182

1183

1184

1185

1186

1187

1188

1189

1190

1191

1192

**1186:** COMPANY: Chase Design Group / CLIENT: Westmont College Athletics / DESIGNER: Margo Chase / ART DIRECTOR: Margo Chase
**1187:** COMPANY: Enhive Creative Studio Pvt. Ltd. / CLIENT: Logan Lacombe / DESIGNER: Debashis Nayak / ART DIRECTOR: Debashis Nayak
**1188:** COMPANY: Dotzero Design / CLIENT: Live Wire Radio / DESIGNER: Jon Wippich, Karen Wippich / ART DIRECTORS: Jon Wippich, Karen Wippich
**1189:** COMPANY: Gardner Design / CLIENT: Classic Media / DESIGNER: Brian Miller / ART DIRECTOR: Brian Miller
**1190:** COMPANY: Gardner Design / CLIENT: Lavish / DESIGNER: Brian Miller / ART DIRECTOR: Brian Miller
**1191:** COMPANY: Gardner Design / CLIENT: Bluebird Books / DESIGNER: Brian Miller / ART DIRECTOR: Brian Miller
**1192:** COMPANY: Gardner Design / CLIENT: Hustler Mowers / DESIGNER: Bill Gardner / ART DIRECTOR: Bill Gardner

1193

1194

1195

1196

1197

1198

Equilibrium Capital

1199

1200

1193: COMPANY: Gardner Design / CLIENT: Marquee Performing Arts Center / DESIGNER: Adam Anderson / ART DIRECTOR: Brian Miller
1194: COMPANY: Gyula Németh / DESIGNER: Gyula Németh
1195: COMPANY: Gardner Design / CLIENT: NexStep / DESIGNER: Brian Weins / ART DIRECTOR: Brian Miller
1196: COMPANY: Gyula Németh / DESIGNER: Gyula Németh
1197: COMPANY: Gardner Design / CLIENT: Tops / DESIGNER: Brian Weins / ART DIRECTOR: Brian Miller
1198: COMPANY: Gyula Németh / DESIGNER: Gyula Németh
1199: COMPANY: Gee + Chung Design / CLIENT: Equilibrium Capital / DESIGNER: Earl Gee / ART DIRECTOR: Earl Gee
1200: COMPANY: Gyula Németh / CLIENT: / DESIGNER: Gyula Németh

1201

1202

1203

1204

1205

1206

1207

1208

**1201:** COMPANY: Gyula Németh / DESIGNER: Gyula Németh
**1202:** COMPANY: Flight Deck Creative / CLIENT: Coppell Farmers Market / DESIGNER: Jason Rahn / ART DIRECTOR: Jason Rahn
**1203:** COMPANY: The Joe Bosack Graphic Design Co. / DESIGNER: Joe Bosack / ART DIRECTOR: Joe Bosack
**1204:** COMPANY: The Joe Bosack Graphic Design Co. / DESIGNER: Joe Bosack / ART DIRECTOR: Joe Bosack
**1205:** COMPANY: Joseph Blalock Design Office / CLIENT: Biz Stylist / DESIGNER: Joseph Blalock
**1206:** COMPANY: Jon Flaming Design / CLIENT: Judd Review / DESIGNER: Jon Flaming / ART DIRECTOR: Jon Flaming
**1207:** COMPANY: Logo Planet Laboratory / CLIENT: Heritage at Kentuscany / DESIGNER: Jeffrey Mardis
**1208:** COMPANY: Joseph Blalock Design Office / CLIENT: Dugan Custom Hot Rods / DESIGNER: Joseph Blalock

2010

1209

1210

GOD BLESS AMERICA

1211

PIG&FINCH gastropub

1212

MARION COUNTY FAIR

1213

1214

1215

**1209:** COMPANY: Joseph Blalock Design Office / CLIENT: Green Horse Financial Consulting / DESIGNER: Joseph Blalock / ART DIRECTOR: Adam Dolch
**1210:** COMPANY: J Sayles Design Co. / CLIENT: West End Arts District / DESIGNER: John Sayles / ART DIRECTOR: John Sayles
**1211:** COMPANY: leightonhubbell.com / CLIENT: Self-Promotion / DESIGNER: Leighton Hubbell / ART DIRECTOR: Leighton Hubbell
**1212:** COMPANY: J Sayles Design Co. / CLIENT: Pig & Finch / DESIGNER: John Sayles / ART DIRECTOR: John Sayles
**1213:** COMPANY: J Sayles Design Co. / CLIENT: Marion County / DESIGNER: John Sayles / ART DIRECTOR: John Sayles
**1214:** COMPANY: Joseph Blalock Design Office / CLIENT: James Plant Racecars / DESIGNER: Joseph Blalock
**1215:** COMPANY: Joseph Blalock Design Office / CLIENT: State of Texas / DESIGNER: Joseph Blalock

 **ARCCON** CONSTRUCTION

1216

1217

1218

1219

1220

1221

**1216:** COMPANY: Base Art Co. / CLIENT: Arccon Construction / DESIGNER: Terry Rohrback / ART DIRECTOR: Terry Rohrback
**1217:** COMPANY: leightonhubbell.com / CLIENT: Axene Industries / DESIGNER: Leighton Hubbell / ART DIRECTOR: Leighton Hubbell
**1218:** COMPANY: leightonhubbell.com / CLIENT: Nectar Labs / DESIGNER: Leighton Hubbell / ART DIRECTOR: Leighton Hubbell
**1219:** COMPANY: leightonhubbell.com / CLIENT: Motive Group / DESIGNER: Leighton Hubbell / ART DIRECTOR: Leighton Hubbell
**1220:** COMPANY: leightonhubbell.com / CLIENT: Pipeline Digital Media / DESIGNER: Leighton Hubbell / ART DIRECTOR: Leighton Hubbell
**1221:** COMPANY: J Sayles Design Co. / CLIENT: Panteleakis Family / DESIGNER: John Sayles / ART DIRECTOR: John Sayles

# Logo Gallery

1222

1223

1224

1225

1226

1227

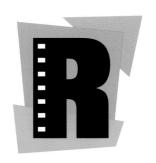

1228

1229

**1222:** COMPANY: leightonhubbell.com / CLIENT: Oney Rooding / DESIGNER: Leighton Hubbell / ART DIRECTOR: Leighton Hubbell
**1223:** COMPANY: Design Center, Inc. / CLIENT: 401k Latte / DESIGNER: Sherwin Schwartzrock
**1224:** COMPANY: leightonhubbell.com / CLIENT: Port of Long Beach / DESIGNER: Leighton Hubbell / ART DIRECTOR: Leighton Hubbell
**1225:** COMPANY: Weather Control / CLIENT: chorosynthesis / DESIGNER: Josh Oakley
**1226:** COMPANY: Pollard Design / DESIGNER: Jeff Pollard
**1227:** COMPANY: Varsity Mascot Company / CLIENT: Palm Beach Atlantic University / DESIGNER: John Nissen / ART DIRECTOR: Dave Adamson
**1228:** COMPANY: Pollard Design / DESIGNER: Jeff Pollard
**1229:** COMPANY: Varsity Mascot Company / CLIENT: Cascade High School / DESIGNERS: Sam Sedor, Wendel Hayes, Ryan Welty / ART DIRECTOR: Dave Adamson

1230

1231

1232

1233

1234

1235

1236

1237

**1230:** COMPANY: H2 Design of Texas / CLIENT: Specs Wine & Spirits Finer Foods / DESIGNER: Hoyt Haffelder / ART DIRECTOR: Hoyt Haffelder
**1231:** COMPANY: ACTUART LP / CLIENT: mayhemstyle / DESIGNER: Peter Vasvari / ART DIRECTOR: Peter Vasvari
**1232:** COMPANY: Star Group / CLIENT: AMNRL / DESIGNER: Scott Oeschger / ART DIRECTOR: Scott Oeschger
**1233:** COMPANY: Ramp / CLIENT: Cambria Inns / DESIGNER: Michael Stinson / ART DIRECTOR: Michael Stinson
**1234:** COMPANY: J. Sayles Design Co. / CLIENT: Beaverdale Neighborhood / DESIGNER: John Sayles / ART DIRECTOR: John Sayles
**1235:** COMPANY: Voov Ltd. / CLIENT: Zsigmond Király Főiskola / DESIGNER: Bálint Egyed / ART DIRECTOR: Bálint Egyed
**1236:** COMPANY: Luke Despatie & The Design Firm / CLIENT: Colony Coffee / DESIGNER: Luke Despatie / ART DIRECTOR: Luke Despatie
**1237:** COMPANY: ACTUART LP / CLIENT: Eula Palmer / DESIGNER: Peter Vasvari / ART DIRECTOR: Peter Vasvari

**FIRM:** THINKING CAP DESIGN CO.
**DESIGNER / ILLUSTRATOR:** KELLY D LAWRENCE
**ART DIRECTOR:** KELLY D LAWRENCE
**CLIENT:** THE GO-GO'S

The Go-Go's were looking to update the tour merchandise for their 2012 tour. What started out as a few shirt ideas morphed into a tour icon/logo as well. The Kali Goddess logo came about during the design process. After reviewing some concepts, Kathy Valentine (bass guitarist) mentioned that they should have an "official" Go-Go's Tour logo. I was hesitant to show them a rough inspired by the Kali myth, as it was a departure from their normal brand. But, it was exactly what they wanted. The icon was perfect for branding the over-all tour and equally represented all five women in the band. Jane Wiedlin (guitarist) had some really interesting fabric swatches with vibrant color pairings that influenced our final color choices.

During the tour there was a bomb threat at a hotel where the Go-Go's were staying and the entire hotel was evacuated. Without their personal belongings (make-up or stage clothes) the ladies went to the local drugstore and loaded up on supplies and then performed the concert wearing their own Go-Go's tour shirts!

*It's refreshing to see creative clients participate in the design process, especially when your color choices are being suggested by Jane Wiedlin, songwriter of a couple of the world's best pop songs of all time.*

*The Kali-Goddess logo direction might at first seem a bit risky, too foreign, or off target. However, the hand-drawn swashy type, retro flip hairdo, and musical instruments in the hands pull it firmly into American pop music appeal.*

*The sketch process was exhaustive. There are so many great options and combinations here; I'm not sure how anyone could have settled on a final solution.*

*This mark has the perfect level of detail. It shrinks down to the size of a guitar pick, yet still has enough visual interest to stand alone on the front of a T-shirt without any additional help.*

Concert photo: courtesy Peer Dollinger

# Logo Gallery

**FLUKE PRESS**

1238

MESA · ARIZ · BE GOOD TO THE MONKEY AND HE'LL BE GOOD TO YOU

1239

## Green Cargo Container
### Environmental Achievement

1240

1241

**CCAD MINDSHOP**

1242

TEX-MEX **EL FENIX** EXPRESS

1243

*Kimberly Wylie*
FINE ART PORTRAITURE

1244

**1238:** COMPANY: Art Chantry Design / CLIENT: Maire Masco / DESIGNER: Art Chantry / ART DIRECTOR: Art Chantry
**1239:** COMPANY: Darwin Avenue / CLIENT: Eclectic Monkey Emporium / DESIGNER: Jason Johnson / ART DIRECTOR: Jason Johnson
**1240:** COMPANY: leightonhubbell.com / CLIENT: Port of Long Beach / DESIGNER: Leighton Hubbell / ART DIRECTOR: Leighton Hubbell
**1241:** COMPANY: Gardner Design / CLIENT: The Church of the Latter Day Saints / DESIGNER: Brian Miller / ART DIRECTOR: Brian Miller
**1242:** COMPANY: Base Art Co. / CLIENT: Columbus College of Art & Design / DESIGNERS: Drue Dixon, Meredith Reuter, Terry Rohrbach / ART DIRECTOR: Terry Rohrback
**1243:** COMPANY: Banowetz & Company / CLIENT: El Fenix Tex-Mex Express / DESIGNER: Kris Murphy / ART DIRECTOR: Eric Venegas
**1244:** COMPANY: Banowetz & Company / CLIENT: Eric Venegas / DESIGNER: Eric Venegas / ART DIRECTOR: Eric Venegas

DOT LAUNCH
EMPOWERING DESIGN ENTREPRENEURS

1245

1246

1247

SKY FISH
ENERGY

1248

1249

1250

1251

**1245:** COMPANY: Gee + Chung Design / CLIENT: Art Center College of Design / DESIGNER: Earl Gee / ART DIRECTOR: Earl Gee
**1246:** COMPANY: Logo Planet Laboratory / CLIENT: Evolve Group / DESIGNER: Jeffrey Mardis
**1247:** COMPANY: Mode Design / CLIENT: Tracy Center for the ARts / DESIGNER: Hans Bennewitz / ART DIRECTOR: Hans Bennewitz
**1248:** COMPANY: Greteman Group / CLIENT: Skyfish Energy / DESIGNER: Landon Barton / ART DIRECTOR: Sonia Greteman
**1249:** COMPANY: Greteman Group / CLIENT: Wichita AeroClub / DESIGNER: Garrett Fresh / ART DIRECTOR: Sonia Greteman
**1250:** COMPANY: Mode Design / CLIENT: Joel Sandvos / DESIGNER: Hans Bennewitz / ART DIRECTOR: Hans Bennewitz
**1251:** COMPANY: Flight Deck Creative / CLIENT: Texas Frightmare Weekend / DESIGNER: Jason Rahn / ART DIRECTOR: Jason Rahn

1252

1253

1254

1255

1256

1257

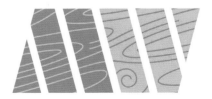

1258

1259

**1252:** COMPANY: The Joe Bosack Graphic Design Co. / DESIGNER: Joe Bosack / ART DIRECTOR: Joe Bosack
**1253:** COMPANY: The Joe Bosack Graphic Design Co. / DESIGNER: Joe Bosack / ART DIRECTOR: Joe Bosack
**1254:** COMPANY: The Joe Bosack Graphic Design Co. / DESIGNER: Joe Bosack / ART DIRECTOR: Joe Bosack
**1255:** COMPANY: Joseph Blalock Design Office / CLIENT: Trophy Hunting Systems / DESIGNER: Joseph Blalock
**1256:** COMPANY: Joseph Blalock Design Office / CLIENT: Bacara Resort & Spa / DESIGNER: Joseph Blalock
**1257:** COMPANY: Joseph Blalock Design Office / CLIENT: Ralph Smyth Entertainment / DESIGNER: Joseph Blalock
**1258:** COMPANY: Joseph Blalock Design Office / CLIENT: Joseph Blalock Design Office / DESIGNER: Joseph Blalock
**1259:** COMPANY: Joseph Blalock Design Office / CLIENT: Moe's Woodworking / DESIGNER: Joseph Blalock

1260

1261

1262

VITTORIO MARZOLA
BOOKS

1263

1264

1265

1266

1267

**1260:** COMPANY: J Sayles Design Co. / CLIENT: Panteleakis Family / DESIGNER: John Sayles / ART DIRECTOR: John Sayles
**1261:** COMPANY: Art Chantry Design / CLIENT: Robert O'Neill, Banc Press / DESIGNER: Art Chantry / ART DIRECTOR: Art Chantry
**1262:** COMPANY: Kris Bazen Creative / CLIENT: Ray's Smokehouse BBQ, Norman, OK / DESIGNER: Kris Bazen / ART DIRECTOR: Kris Bazen
**1263:** COMPANY: Lanky Design / CLIENT: Vittorio Marzola Books / DESIGNER: Giancarlo Salvador / ART DIRECTOR: Giancarlo Salvador
**1264:** COMPANY: leightonhubbell.com / CLIENT: Navigator Group / DESIGNER: Leighton Hubbell / ART DIRECTOR: Leighton Hubbell
**1265:** COMPANY: Neu Creative, LLC / CLIENT: Columbia Hobby Distribution / DESIGNER: Marc Neidlinger / ART DIRECTOR: Marc Neidlinger
**1266:** COMPANY: Gravitate Design Studio / CLIENT: / DESIGNER: Marc Neidlinger / ART DIRECTOR: Marc Neidlinger
**1267:** COMPANY: Michael Doret Graphic Design / CLIENT: Canter's Deli / DESIGNER: Michael Doret / ART DIRECTOR: Bonnie Bloomgarden

1268

1269

1270

1271

1272

1273

1274

# Quaint CO.

1275

1276

1277

1279

1278

1280

**1275:** COMPANY: Jeremy Slagle Graphic Design / CLIENT: Quaint Co. / DESIGNER: Jeremy Slagle / ART DIRECTOR: Jeremy Slagle
**1276:** CLIENT: Fleur De Links / DESIGNER: Jude Landry
**1277:** COMPANY: Salvadore Anguiano / CLIENT: Imaginarios Software Development / DESIGNER: Salvadore Anguiano / ART DIRECTOR: Salvadore Anguiano
**1278:** COMPANY: Pollard Design / DESIGNER: Jeff Pollard
**1279:** COMPANY: Jeremy Slagle Graphic Design / CLIENT: Teodora's Kitchen / DESIGNER: Jeremy Slagle / ART DIRECTOR: Jeremy Slagle
**1280:** DESIGNER: Floris Voorveld

1281

1282

1283

1284

1285

1286

**Arizona Lottery**

1287

**VISION FOR THE Future**

1288

**1281:** COMPANY: Throttle Design Mechanics / CLIENT: Pharaohs Street Rodders / DESIGNER: John Nissen / ART DIRECTOR: Dave Adamson
**1282:** COMPANY: Weather Control / CLIENT: Eddie Bauer / DESIGNER: Josh Oakley
**1283:** COMPANY: Varsity Mascot Company / CLIENT: Salem Academy High School / DESIGNERS: Sam Sedor, Wendel Hayes / ART DIRECTOR: Dave Adamson
**1284:** COMPANY: Chase Design Group / CLIENT: The CW / DESIGNER: Larimie Garcia / ART DIRECTOR: Margo Chase
**1285:** COMPANY: Timber Design Co. / DESIGNER: Lars Lawson
**1286:** COMPANY: Superbig Creative / CLIENT: Jones Soda / DESIGNER: Josh Oakley / ART DIRECTOR: Kevin Walsh
**1287:** COMPANY: R&R Partners / CLIENT: Arizona Lottery / DESIGNER: Randy Heil / ART DIRECTOR: Randy Heil
**1288:** COMPANY: Weather Control / CLIENT: Sustainable Harvest / DESIGNER: Josh Oakley

1289

1290

1291

1292

1293

1294

1295

1296

**1289:** COMPANY: Clay McIntosh Creative / CLIENT: Sunny Side Up Cafe / DESIGNER: Clay McIntosh / ART DIRECTOR: Clay McIntosh
**1290:** COMPANY: Star Group / CLIENT: AMNRL / DESIGNER: Scott Oeschger / ART DIRECTOR: Scott Oeschger
**1291:** COMPANY: R&R Partners / CLIENT: Las Vegas Convention & Visitors Authority / DESIGNER: Randy Heil / ART DIRECTOR: Randy Heil
**1292:** COMPANY: H2 Design of Texas / CLIENT: John Burroughs School / DESIGNER: Hoyt Haffelder / ART DIRECTOR: Hoyt Haffelder
**1293:** COMPANY: R&R Partners / CLIENT: R&R Partners / DESIGNER: Randy Heil / ART DIRECTOR: Randy Heil
**1294:** COMPANY: Mint / CLIENT: Reddington / DESIGNER: Bryan Danknich, Mike Calkins / ART DIRECTOR: Mike Calkins
**1295:** COMPANY: Mint / CLIENT: Adidas / DESIGNER: Mike Calkins
**1296:** COMPANY: / CLIENT: Luum / DESIGNER: Jacob Carter, Bryan Danknich / ART DIRECTOR: Mike Calkins

# A Closer Look

**FIRM:** GYULA NÉMETH
**DESIGNER / ILLUSTRATOR:** GYULA NÉMETH
**CLIENT:** AMERICAN TAX CEDITS GROUP, INC.

ATG is based out of offices in Los Angeles, Fresno (CA), and Dublin. It specializes in identifying, processing, and implementing custom-tailored tax solutions developed around more than ninety different tax credits and incentive programs offered in the state of California.

ATG was founded upon the notion that any business that qualifies for the government's considerable array of tax incentives deserves access to them whether they are small, owner-operated businesses or large, multinational corporations.

It's always pretty challenging to work for companies like ATG that deal with far more serious business than we designers do. They handle stuff that we can hardly understand. That's one of the reasons why we can approach these projects with bold and clear ideas that help the business simplify their message and reach more possible clientele.

*The carefully planned balance of positive to negative space in this logo allows it to be used as a "supergraphic" on various pieces of business collateral. Also, if this logo were any less detailed, it wouldn't have worked as well.*

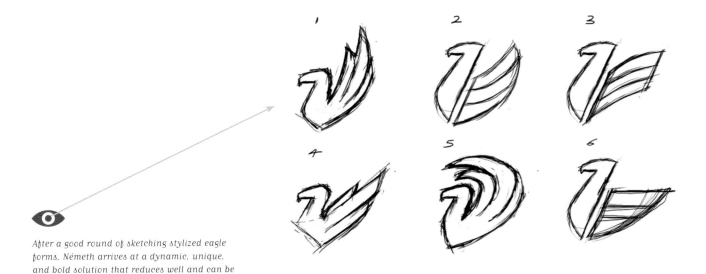

*After a good round of sketching stylized eagle forms, Németh arrives at a dynamic, unique, and bold solution that reduces well and can be reproduced with one color—not an easy task.*

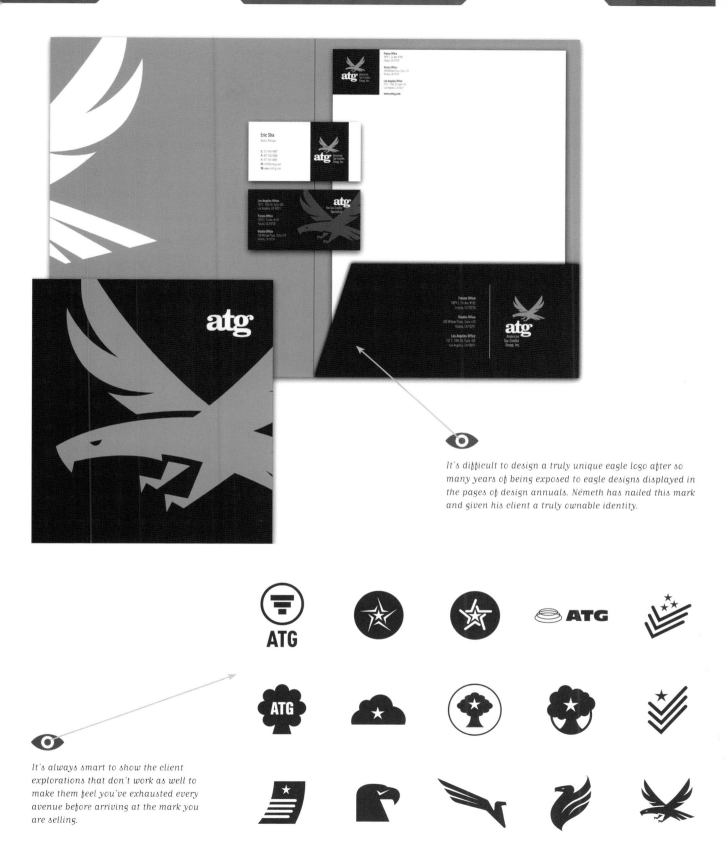

It's difficult to design a truly unique eagle logo after so many years of being exposed to eagle designs displayed in the pages of design annuals. Németh has nailed this mark and given his client a truly ownable identity.

It's always smart to show the client explorations that don't work as well to make them feel you've exhausted every avenue before arriving at the mark you are selling.

1297

1298

1299

1300

1301

1302

1303

**1297:** COMPANY: Adam Anderson / DESIGNER: Adam Anderson
**1298:** COMPANY: Art Chantry Design / CLIENT: One Louder Records / DESIGNER: Art Chantry / ART DIRECTOR: Art Chantry
**1299:** COMPANY: Adam Anderson / DESIGNER: Adam Anderson
**1300:** COMPANY: atomicvibe / CLIENT: atomicvibe, graphic design studio / DESIGNER: Jon Stapp / ART DIRECTOR: Jon Stapp
**1301:** COMPANY: Banowetz & Company / CLIENT: Grain / Restaurant / Bar / DESIGNER: Lily Smith+Kirkley / ART DIRECTOR: Eric Venegas
**1302:** COMPANY: Chase Design Group / CLIENT: The CW / DESIGNER: Jon Ariazza, Larimie Garcia / ART DIRECTOR: Margo Chase
**1303:** COMPANY: Banowetz & Company / CLIENT: Pro Soap / DESIGNER: Sarah Terrell / ART DIRECTOR: Eric Venegas

**REBLOOM UPTOWN**

1304

**GRACE HILL**
· WINERY ·

1305

1306

1307

 **a lovely note™**

1308

CCAD **MINDSHOP**

1309

1310

**1304:** COMPANY: Miles Design / CLIENT: Carreau Design / DESIGNER: Joshua Cook
**1305:** COMPANY: Gardner Design / CLIENT: Grace Hill Winery / DESIGNER: Luke Bott / ART DIRECTOR: Brian Miller
**1306:** COMPANY: Chase Design Group / CLIENT: Couture Colour, LLC / DESIGNERS: Margo Chase, Paula Hansanugrum / ART DIRECTOR: Margo Chase
**1307:** CLIENT: Restaurant Industry / DESIGNER: Chris Parks / ART DIRECTOR: Chris Parks
**1308:** COMPANY: Jared Granger / CLIENT: A Lovely Note / DESIGNER: Jared Granger / ART DIRECTOR: Jared Granger
**1309:** COMPANY: Base Art Co. / CLIENT: Columbus College of Art & Design / DESIGNERS: Drue Dixon, Meredith Reuter, Terry Rohrbach / ART DIRECTOR: Terry Rohrbach
**1310:** COMPANY: Art Chantry Design / CLIENT: Amy McBride, City of Tacoma / DESIGNER: Art Chantry / ART DIRECTOR: Art Chantry

HIGHBRIDGE
*Management*

1311

1312

*trade* mark

1313

1314

SIGNATURE
TAILWINS™

1315

SPAY·NEUTER
KANSAS

1316

1317

1318

**1311:** COMPANY: Gardner Design / CLIENT: Highbridge Management / DESIGNER: Adam Anderson / ART DIRECTOR: Brian Miller
**1312:** COMPANY: Gardner Design / CLIENT: Lavish / DESIGNER: Brian Miller / ART DIRECTOR: Brian Miller
**1313:** COMPANY: Gardner Design / CLIENT: Mega Metals / DESIGNER: Chris Parks / ART DIRECTOR: Brian Miller
**1314:** COMPANY: Gardner Design / CLIENT: Neighborhood Entrepreneur / DESIGNER: Bill Gardner / ART DIRECTOR: Bill Gardner
**1315:** COMPANY: Greteman Group / CLIENT: Signature Flight Support / DESIGNER: Chris Parks / ART DIRECTOR: Sonia Greteman
**1316:** COMPANY: Greteman Group / CLIENT: Spay|Neuter KS / DESIGNER: Chris Parks / ART DIRECTOR: Sonia Greteman
**1317:** COMPANY: Gyula Németh / DESIGNER: Gyula Németh
**1318:** COMPANY: Gyula Németh / DESIGNER: Gyula Németh

1319

1320

1321

1322

1323

1324

1325

1326

1319: COMPANY: Joseph Blalock Design Office / CLIENT: James Plant Racecars / DESIGNER: Joseph Blalock
1320: COMPANY: Joseph Blalock Design Office / CLIENT: State of Texas / DESIGNER: Joseph Blalock
1321: COMPANY: Art Chantry Design / CLIENT: The Trucadeno / DESIGNER: Art Chantry / ART DIRECTOR: Art Chantry
1322: COMPANY: J Sayles Design Co. / CLIENT: Panteleakis Family / DESIGNER: John Sayles / ART DIRECTOR: John Sayles
1323: COMPANY: The Joe Bosack Graphic Design Co. / DESIGNER: Joe Bosack / ART DIRECTOR: Joe Bosack
1324: COMPANY: Logo Planet Laboratory / CLIENT: Dedulcibus / DESIGNER: Jeffrey Mardis
1325: COMPANY: Hatch Design / CLIENT: Specialty's Cafe and Bakery / DESIGNER: Eszter Clark / ART DIRECTORS: Joel Templin, Katie Jain
1326: COMPANY: Bailey Lauerman / CLIENT: ScreenInk / DESIGNER: James Strange / ART DIRECTOR: James Strange

1328

1329

1327

1330

1331

1332

1333

**1327:** COMPANY: Greteman Group / CLIENT: Real Men Real Horses / DESIGNER: Ty Wilkins / ART DIRECTOR: Sonia Greteman
**1328:** COMPANY: The Mahoney Studio / CLIENT: Ice Cream Social / DESIGNERS: Trish Mahoney, Patrick Mahoney / ART DIRECTOR: Trish Mahoney
**1329:** COMPANY: Pollard Design / DESIGNER: Jeff Pollard
**1330:** COMPANY: leightonhubbell.com / CLIENT: Do Good Things / DESIGNER: Leighton Hubbell / ART DIRECTOR: Leighton Hubbell
**1331:** COMPANY: Sean Heisler / CLIENT: Whitman Consulting Group / DESIGNER: Sean Heisler / ART DIRECTOR: Sean Heisler
**1332:** COMPANY: Banowetz & Company / CLIENT: St John's Episcopal School / DESIGNER: Lily Smith+Kirkley / ART DIRECTOR: Eric Venegas
**1333:** COMPANY: Pollard Design / DESIGNER: Jeff Pollard

KIMBERLY WYLIE

FINE ART PORTRAITURE

1334

AROMAS
· AVES ·

1335

1336

beverage partners
worldwide

1337

;-*
;

simply kissable
LIP BALM

1338

1339

**1334:** COMPANY: Banowetz & Company / CLIENT: Kimberly Wylie / Photography / DESIGNER: Sarah Terrell / ART DIRECTOR: Eric Venegas
**1335:** COMPANY: Salvadore Anguiano / CLIENT: Aromas Restaurant / DESIGNER: Salvadore Anguiano / ART DIRECTOR: Salvadore Anguiano
**1336:** COMPANY: Thrillustrate
**1337:** COMPANY: Office / CLIENT: BPW / DESIGNER: Office / ART DIRECTOR: Jason Schulte
**1338:** COMPANY: Lewis Communications / CLIENT: Simply Kissable Lip Balm / DESIGNER: Robert Froedge / ART DIRECTOR: Robert Froedge
**1339:** COMPANY: M3AD.com / CLIENT: Chronos / DESIGNER: Dan McElhattan III / ART DIRECTOR: Dan McElhattan III

1340

1341

1342

1343

1344

1345

1346

1347

1340: COMPANY: Gardner Design / CLIENT: Building Controls and Services, Inc. / DESIGNER: Adam Anderson / ART DIRECTOR: Brian Miller
1341: COMPANY: Schwartzrock Graphic Arts / CLIENT: TorqueTec / DESIGNER: Sherwin Schwartzrock
1342: COMPANY: Schwartzrock Graphic Arts / CLIENT: Pugleasa Company / DESIGNER: Sherwin Schwartzrock
1343: COMPANY: Gardner Design / CLIENT: Collins Bus Corporation / DESIGNER: Luke Bott / ART DIRECTOR: Brian Miller
1344: COMPANY: Mattson Creative / DESIGNER: Ty Mattson
1345: COMPANY: Schwartzrock Graphic Arts / CLIENT: St. Bonifacious Fire Dept. / DESIGNER: Sherwin Schwartzrock
1346: COMPANY: Schwartzrock Graphic Arts / CLIENT: Wiese Comminications / DESIGNER: Sherwin Schwartzrock
1347: COMPANY: Schwartzrock Graphic Arts / CLIENT: Derek Derfus / DESIGNER: Sherwin Schwartzrock

1348

1349

1350

1351

1352

1353

1354

1355

**1348:** COMPANY: chameleon design / CLIENT: Jennifer Green / DESIGNER: Tomas Vateha / ART DIRECTOR: Tomas Vateha
**1349:** COMPANY: ACTUART LP / CLIENT: Eagle Mountain Capital, Ltd. / DESIGNER: Peter Vasvari / ART DIRECTOR: Peter Vasvari
**1350:** COMPANY: Schwartzrock Graphic Arts / CLIENT: FSC / DESIGNER: Sherwin Schwartzrock
**1351:** COMPANY: Robert Finkel Design / CLIENT: Town Treats / DESIGNER: Robert Finkel / ART DIRECTOR: Robert Finkel
**1352:** COMPANY: Invisible Creature / CLIENT: Artist Series Guitar / DESIGNER: Ryan Clark / ART DIRECTOR: Ryan Clark
**1353:** COMPANY: M&M / CLIENT: M&M / DESIGNER: Scott Oeschger / ART DIRECTOR: Scott Oeschger
**1354:** COMPANY: M&M / CLIENT: M&M / DESIGNER: Scott Oeschger / ART DIRECTOR: Scott Oeschger
**1355:** COMPANY: Janus / CLIENT: Nature's Kitchen / DESIGNER: Aleksandar Petrovic / ART DIRECTOR: Aleksandar Petrovic

**FIRM:** MATTSON CREATIVE
**DESIGNER / ILLUSTRATOR:** TY MATTSON
**ART DIRECTOR:** TY MATTSON
**CLIENT:** POCONO MODERN

With attention to detail and a commitment to sustainable practices, Pocono Modern is building homes in the Poconos with a fresh, modern twist.

Pocono Modern is the vision of Kraig Kalashian, who is an incredible architect and designer, which makes all of our collaborations very creative. He has a great eye for design and we tend to gravitate toward the same aesthetic, which is fun.

In the final solution, the Pocono Mountains are represented, but are abstracted into simple, strong shapes. There is some interesting positive/negative space created in the middle of the mark by the intersection of the angles. The wood texture evokes the organic nature of the Poconos, and the color fields represent the minimal, modern aspect of the brand.

*I don't care what you say, working fast and loose in a sketchbook and fleshing out ideas prior to building logo forms on a computer will always make your concepts stronger and your rendering more refined in a shorter amount of time. It's also a great way to visually communicate with a client before heading down a road he or she is unwilling to travel.*

*Preliminary exploration sells geometric retro, post-modern idealism, coupled with timeless typefaces. The fresh color palettes keep this mark from feeling too dated.*

The triangle shapes were the perfect elements to represent the Pocono Mountains. The forms also replicated wonderfully as a decorative pattern to be used on packaging and stationery. The sparse type treatments kept the whole identity package feeling appropriately modern.

1356

## EMONA HOUSE

LUXUSHEIM FÜR SENIOREN

1357

1358

## THREE NUTS
GENERAL CONTRACTORS

1359

ADD WATER. GET CLEAN.

1360

1361

1362

**1356:** COMPANY: Adam Anderson / DESIGNER: Adam Anderson
**1357:** CLIENT: Emona House / DESIGNER: Julian Hrankov
**1358:** COMPANY: A3 Design / CLIENT: Carmel C.C. / DESIGNER: Alan Altman / ART DIRECTOR: Amanda Altman
**1359:** COMPANY: atomicvibe / CLIENT: Three Nuts General Contractors / DESIGNER: Jon Stapp / ART DIRECTOR: Jon Stapp
**1360:** COMPANY: Banowetz & Company / CLIENT: Pro Soap / DESIGNER: Eric Venegas / ART DIRECTOR: Eric Venegas
**1361:** COMPANY: Design Center, Inc. / CLIENT: Design Center, Inc. / DESIGNER: Sherwin Schwartzrock / ART DIRECTOR: John Reger
**1362:** COMPANY: Base Art Co. / CLIENT: Investing in Workers / DESIGNER: Terry Rohrback / ART DIRECTOR: Terry Rohrback

1363

*BLUEBIRD*
EST. 2012
BOOKS

1364

**Wee** *Little* **Whale**

1365

trade mark
BELABUMBUM
LINGERIE & MATERNITY
• FOUNDED IN 2001 •

1366

**alebrijes**mexicancuisine

1367

1368

SCENE on MAIN
urban.cocktails.cuisine.

1369

**1363:** COMPANY: Adam Anderson / DESIGNER: Adam Anderson
**1364:** COMPANY: Gardner Design / CLIENT: Bluebird Books / DESIGNER: Adam Anderson / ART DIRECTOR: Brian Miller
**1365:** COMPANY: Adam Anderson / DESIGNER: Adam Anderson
**1366:** COMPANY: Gardner Design / CLIENT: Bella Bum Bum / DESIGNER: Brian Miller / ART DIRECTOR: Brian Miller
**1367:** COMPANY: pizelato immagine corporativa™ / CLIENT: alebrijes mexican cuisine / DESIGNER: ivan abbadie / ART DIRECTOR: ivan abbadie
**1368:** COMPANY: Owen Jones Design / CLIENT: Private client tattoo design / DESIGNER: Owen Jones / ART DIRECTOR: Owen Jones
**1369:** COMPANY: Banowetz & Company / CLIENT: Scene on Main / DESIGNER: Lily Smith+Kirkley / ART DIRECTOR: Eric Venegas

1370

1371

1372

1373

1374

1375

1376

1377

**1370:** COMPANY: Gardner Design / CLIENT: Graphic Impressions / DESIGNER: Luke Bott / ART DIRECTOR: Brian Miller
**1371:** COMPANY: Gardner Design / CLIENT: Marquee Performing Arts Center / DESIGNER: Adam Anderson / ART DIRECTOR: Brian Miller
**1372:** COMPANY: Gardner Design / CLIENT: KETCH / DESIGNER: Adam Anderson / ART DIRECTOR: Brian Miller
**1373:** COMPANY: Gardner Design / CLIENT: Reno / DESIGNER: Chris Parks / ART DIRECTOR: Brian Miller
**1374:** COMPANY: Gardner Design / CLIENT: Bluebird Books / DESIGNER: Adam Anderson / ART DIRECTOR: Brian Miller
**1375:** COMPANY: Gardner Design / CLIENT: Parkstone at College Hill / DESIGNER: Brian Miller / ART DIRECTOR: Brian Miller
**1376:** COMPANY: WORKtoDATE (www.worktodate.com) / CLIENT: Harvest Moon Farms / DESIGNER: Greg Bennett / ART DIRECTOR: Greg Bennett
**1377:** COMPANY: Gardner Design / CLIENT: Mystik Butterfly / DESIGNER: Brian Miller / ART DIRECTOR: Brian Miller

1378

1379

1380

1381

1382

1383

1384

1385

**1378:** COMPANY: Greteman Group / CLIENT: Hutton Construction / DESIGNER: Chris Parks / ART DIRECTOR: Sonia Greteman
**1379:** COMPANY: Gyula Németh / DESIGNER: Gyula Németh
**1380:** COMPANY: Hatch Design / CLIENT: JAQK Cellars / DESIGNERS: Eszter Clark, Ryan Meis / ART DIRECTORS: Joel Templin, Katie Jain
**1381:** COMPANY: Gyula Németh / CLIENT: / DESIGNER: Gyula Németh
**1382:** COMPANY: Hatch Design / CLIENT: Segrams / DESIGNER: Eszter Clark / ART DIRECTORS: Joel Templin, Katie Jain
**1383:** COMPANY: Jay Vigon Design / CLIENT: Jerry's Home / DESIGNER: Jay Vigon / ART DIRECTOR: Jay Vigon
**1384:** COMPANY: Holy Cow Creative / CLIENT: Hope Church / DESIGNER: Von Glitshka / ART DIRECTOR: Michael Buckingham
**1385:** COMPANY: Jake Thompson / CLIENT: Epiphanie Co. / DESIGNER: Jake Thompson / ART DIRECTOR: Jake Thompson

SCOTT **M** ONT GoM ERY *Photography*

1386

NOUSUON

1387

1388

south shore
dental prosthetics

1389

1390

1391

1392

**1386:** COMPANY: leightonhubbell.com / CLIENT: Scott Montgomery Photography / DESIGNER: Leighton Hubbell / ART DIRECTOR: Leighton Hubbell
**1387:** COMPANY: leightonhubbell.com / CLIENT: Nousuon / DESIGNER: Leighton Hubbell / ART DIRECTOR: Leighton Hubbell
**1388:** COMPANY: leightonhubbell.com / CLIENT: Nectar Labs / DESIGNER: Leighton Hubbell / ART DIRECTOR: Leighton Hubbell
**1389:** COMPANY: leightonhubbell.com / CLIENT: South Shore Dental Prosthetics / DESIGNER: Leighton Hubbell / ART DIRECTOR: Leighton Hubbell
**1390:** COMPANY: leightonhubbell.com / CLIENT: Motive Group / DESIGNER: Leighton Hubbell / ART DIRECTOR: Leighton Hubbell
**1391:** CLIENT: Self-Promotion / DESIGNER: Jude Landry
**1392:** COMPANY: Design Center, Inc. / CLIENT: ProTech, Inc. / DESIGNER: Sherwin Schwartzrock / ART DIRECTOR: John Reger

1393

UND NURSE ANESTHESIA PROGRAM
THE UNIVERSITY OF NORTH DAKOTA

1394

1395

SOUTH
SHORE
DENTAL PROSTHETICS

1396

1397

effective
communications

1398

**1393:** COMPANY: leightonhubbell.com / CLIENT: TimeDog / DESIGNER: Leighton Hubbell / ART DIRECTOR: Leighton Hubbell
**1394:** COMPANY: leightonhubbell.com / CLIENT: University of North Dakota / DESIGNER: Leighton Hubbell / ART DIRECTOR: Leighton Hubbell
**1395:** COMPANY: Matt Lehman Studio / CLIENT: Make It Bigger Mama Publicity / ART DIRECTORS: Brad Henderson, Stephanie Fields
**1396:** COMPANY: leightonhubbell.com / CLIENT: South Shore Dental Prosthetics / DESIGNER: Leighton Hubbell / ART DIRECTOR: Leighton Hubbell
**1397:** COMPANY: Schwartzrock Graphic Arts / CLIENT: 3.2.1, Inc. / DESIGNER: Sherwin Schwartzrock
**1398:** COMPANY: J Sayles Design Co. / CLIENT: Effective Communication / DESIGNER: John Sayles / ART DIRECTOR: John Sayles

1399

1400

1401

1402

1403

1404

1405

1406

1399: COMPANY: Mirko Ilić Corp. / CLIENT: Kulturni Centar Beograd / DESIGNER: Mirko Ilić / ART DIRECTOR: Mirko Ilić
1400: COMPANY: Timber Design Co. / DESIGNER: Lars Lawson
1401: COMPANY: Sophia Georgopoulou Design / CLIENT: MITERRA - Mother Earth's Finest / DESIGNER: Sophia Georgopoulou / ART DIRECTOR: Sophia Georgopoulou
1402: COMPANY: The Mahoney Studio / CLIENT: Bitty Bakeshop / DESIGNERS: Trish Mahoney, Patrick Mahoney / ART DIRECTOR: Trish Mahoney
1403: COMPANY: Adam Anderson / DESIGNER: Adam Anderson
1404: COMPANY: Salvadore Anguiano / CLIENT: Aromas Restaurant / DESIGNER: Salvadore Anguiano / ART DIRECTOR: Salvadore Anguiano
1405: COMPANY: REACTOR design Studio / CLIENT: Computer Engineering, Inc. / DESIGNERS: Chase Wilson, Samantha Fine / ART DIRECTOR: Clifton Alexander
1406: COMPANY: Ruth Weiler / CLIENT: Kassandra Siebel / DESIGNER: Ruth Weiler / ART DIRECTOR: Ruth Weiler

1407

1408

1409

1410

1411

1412

1413

1414

**1407:** COMPANY: chameleon design / CLIENT: Tomas Vateha / DESIGNER: Tomas Vateha / ART DIRECTOR: Tomas Vateha
**1408:** COMPANY: Weather Control / CLIENT: Rossignol / DESIGNER: Josh Oakley
**1409:** COMPANY: Mint / CLIENT: Gift / DESIGNER: Mike Calkins
**1410:** COMPANY: Schwartzrock Graphic Arts / CLIENT: TorqueTec / DESIGNER: Sherwin Schwartzrock
**1411:** COMPANY: R&R Partners / CLIENT: Lou Ruvo Brain Institute / DESIGNER: Randy Heil / ART DIRECTOR: Randy Heil
**1412:** COMPANY: Holy Cow Creative / CLIENT: Hope Church / DESIGNER: Von Glitshka / ART DIRECTOR: Michael Buckingham
**1413:** COMPANY: Schwartzrock Graphic Arts / CLIENT: Fox River Mills / DESIGNER: Sherwin Schwartzrock
**1414:** COMPANY: Schwartzrock Graphic Arts / CLIENT: RiverBrand Design / DESIGNER: Sherwin Schwartzrock

# A Closer Look

**IN-HOUSE:** ORCHESTRA
**DESIGNERS:** TY WILKINS, BRENT COUCHMAN & RYAN FEERER
**CLIENTS:** GENTRY UNDERWOOD AND SCOTT CANNON

Orchestra is a powerful application combining real-time chat with an elegant to-do list. Founders Gentry Underwood and Scott Cannon assembled a team of three designers from different cities to collaborate on the logo design. The team consisted of Brent Couchman, Ryan Feerer, and Ty Wilkins.

The design team initially explored playful and organic forms with the goal of conveying the approachable and friendly nature of the application. Transparency and overprinting were utilized to combine shapes such as clouds, arrows, buildings, and whales to demonstrate the ease of collaboration. The theme of simplicity was further explored with various interpretations of a magic wand. A plucked petal from a flower represents a wish fulfilled, an arrow underlines efficiency, a bee and his hive suggest the diligence of completing a task, and a check mark and clipboard highlight the core to-do list capability of Orchestra.

Eventually the management team at Orchestra decided that a pivot away from an organic and playful symbol toward a bold, crisp, and minimal solution best fit their goals and target audience. Furthermore, the team felt it was essential that the symbol communicate both of the application's core abilities: chat and list making. The final selected logo has a consistent line weight with a minimal speech bubble that also doubles as an *O* for Orchestra.

*Clean iconic marks are deceptively simple. Taking two common themes yet achieving a unique graphic takes smart thinking and well-crafted execution. has been clearly done here.*

*Fun and color explorations touching on the pedestrian and magical aspects of this product's offerings show the depth of ideas considered.*

Even though the client u-turned at this stage, the end result of the initial exploration arrived at three strong solutions.

*orchestra*

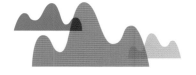

**orchestra**

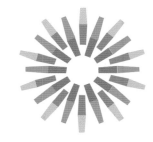

**orchestra**

A diverse collection of speaking-bubble and check-mark variations in a new round of exploratory directions helped the team establish a strong iconic brand while avoiding the pitfalls that usually come with common themes.

STREETSIDE LOUNGE

1415

1416

1417

1418

1419

CELEBRATE.
IMAGINE.

1420

1421

1422

Φ ®

# philab

1423

1424

1425

1426

1427

STUDENT
MINISTRY
HIGH SCHOOL

1428

1422: COMPANY: Adam Anderson / DESIGNER: Adam Anderson
1423: COMPANY: Chris Trivizas / CLIENT: Philab Cosmetics s.a. / DESIGNER: Chris Trivizas / ART DIRECTOR: Chris Trivizas
1424: COMPANY: Invisible Creature / CLIENT: Live Nation / DESIGNER: Ryan Clark / ART DIRECTOR: Ryan Clark
1425: COMPANY: Chris Rooney Illustration/Design / CLIENT: MOG / DESIGNER: Chris Rooney
1426: COMPANY: Brent Couchman Design / CLIENT: Excited Atom / DESIGNER: Brent Couchman
1427: COMPANY: Adam Anderson / DESIGNER: Adam Anderson
1428: COMPANY: Adam Anderson / DESIGNER: Adam Anderson

# Logo Gallery

1429

1430

1431

1432

1433

1434

1435

1436

**1429:** CLIENT: Kaftan Studio / DESIGNER: Muamer ADILOVIC / ART DIRECTOR: Muamer ADILOVIC
**1430:** COMPANY: Gyula Németh / DESIGNER: Gyula Németh
**1431:** COMPANY: Gardner Design / CLIENT: A Little Biz / DESIGNER: Chris Parks / ART DIRECTOR: Brian Miller
**1432:** COMPANY: WORKtoDATE (www.worktodate.com) / CLIENT: Record Breaking Gifts / DESIGNER: Greg Bennett / ART DIRECTOR: Greg Bennett
**1433:** COMPANY: Sophia Georgopoulou Design / CLIENT: Chromatistes Meres, Anthia Vlassopoulou / DESIGNER: Sophia Georgopoulou / ART DIRECTOR: Sophia Georgopoulou
**1434:** COMPANY: Brent Couchman Design / CLIENT: Katie Bowie Photography / DESIGNER: Brent Couchman
**1435:** COMPANY: Gardner Design / CLIENT: The Church of the Latter Day Saints / DESIGNER: Brian Miller / ART DIRECTOR: Brian Miller
**1436:** COMPANY: Gardner Design / CLIENT: Tops / DESIGNER: Brian Weins / ART DIRECTOR: Brian Miller

**bigdog**
productions

1437

1438

1439

1440

PACIFIC
AIRFINANCE

1441

campground.com

1442

1443

CHAMBERS
COUNTY
LOGISTIC
CENTER

1444

**1437:** COMPANY: Flight Deck Creative / CLIENT: Charles Barry / DESIGNER: Jason Rahn / ART DIRECTOR: Jason Rahn
**1438:** COMPANY: Gardner Design / CLIENT: Grumpy Okd Men / DESIGNER: Bill Gardner / ART DIRECTOR: Bill Gardner
**1439:** COMPANY: Joseph Blalock Design Office / CLIENT: Small Smiles Dental Cemter/GSD&M / DESIGNER: Joseph Blalock
**1440:** COMPANY: Gyula Németh / DESIGNER: Gyula Németh
**1441:** COMPANY: Kim Chan / CLIENT: Pacific Air Finance / DESIGNER: Kim Chan / ART DIRECTOR: Kim Chan
**1442:** COMPANY: leightonhubbell.com / CLIENT: Leisure Interactive / DESIGNER: Leighton Hubbell / ART DIRECTOR: Leighton Hubbell
**1443:** COMPANY: 26am / CLIENT: 7 Sirens Rum / DESIGNER: Hans Bennewitz / ART DIRECTOR: David Sudarma
**1444:** COMPANY: leightonhubbell.com / CLIENT: Chambers County Logistics Center / DESIGNER: Leighton Hubbell / ART DIRECTOR: Leighton Hubbell

1446

1445

1448

1449

1450

1451

**1445:** COMPANY: Sean Heisler / CLIENT: Creedoo / DESIGNER: Sean Heisler / ART DIRECTOR: Sean Heisler
**1446:** COMPANY: Spindletop Design / CLIENT: Smith's Opticians / DESIGNER: Jennifer Blanco / ART DIRECTOR: Jennifer Blanco
**1447:** CLIENT: runbee.ru / DESIGNER: Artem Dvorzhak
**1448:** COMPANY: Pollard Design / DESIGNER: Jeff Pollard
**1449:** COMPANY: Schwartzrock Graphic Arts / CLIENT: Noble Communications / DESIGNER: Sherwin Schwartzrock
**1450:** CLIENT: agrushka.ru / DESIGNER: Artem Dvorzhak
**1451:** COMPANY: Sean Heisler / CLIENT: Beer Garden / DESIGNER: Sean Heisler / ART DIRECTOR: Sean Heisler

1452

la santa
moda pop mexicana

# 20/20
# VISION
## CENTRE LTD (HK)
### 363 NATHAN ROAD
### HANG SHING BLDG #1007
### KOWLOON·HONG KONG
#### TELEPHONE·2332·1841

#### WWW·2020VISION·HK

1453

theCollective

1454

1455

GRAND ST.

1456

1457

**1452:** COMPANY: Bruketa & Zinić OM, Brandoctor / CLIENT: ORYX group / DESIGNER: Neven Crljenak / ART DIRECTOR: Neven Crljenak
**1453:** COMPANY: Salvadore Anguiano / CLIENT: La Santa Clothing / DESIGNER: Salvadore Anguiano / ART DIRECTOR: Salvadore Anguiano
**1454:** COMPANY: Mattson Creative / DESIGNER: Ty Mattson
**1455:** COMPANY: Gee + Chung Design / CLIENT: 20/20 Vision Centre Ltd (HK) / DESIGNER: Earl Gee / ART DIRECTOR: Earl Gee
**1456:** CLIENT: Sedgwick County Zoo / DESIGNER: Chris Parks / ART DIRECTOR: Chris Parks
**1457:** COMPANY: TY Design / CLIENT: Grand St. / DESIGNER: Ty Wilkins / ART DIRECTOR: Ty Wilkins

# Logo Gallery

### ANGR

1458

1459

### lemoviés
KTHMA

1460

1461

UPSTATE **X** NEW YORK
TRADE INSTITUTE

1462

1463

1464

1465

**1458:** COMPANY: Invisible Creature / CLIENT: Ain't No Grave Records / DESIGNER: Ryan Clark / ART DIRECTOR: Ryan Clark
**1459:** COMPANY: Schwartzrock Graphic Arts / CLIENT: Kingstone Media / DESIGNER: Sherwin Schwartzrock
**1460:** COMPANY: Chris Trivizas / CLIENT: Lemonies Estate / DESIGNER: Chris Trivizas / ART DIRECTOR: Chris Trivizas
**1461:** COMPANY: Schwartzrock Graphic Arts / CLIENT: Werner Design Werks / DESIGNER: Sherwin Schwartzrock
**1462:** COMPANY: A3 Design / CLIENT: Upstate New York Trade Institute / DESIGNER: Alan Altman / ART DIRECTOR: Amanda Altman
**1463:** COMPANY: Schwartzrock Graphic Arts / CLIENT: Kurt Kolka / DESIGNER: Sherwin Schwartzrock
**1464:** COMPANY: R&R Partners / CLIENT: MGM Mirage / DESIGNER: Randy Heil / ART DIRECTOR: Randy Heil
**1465:** COMPANY: Jeff Fisher LogoMotives / CLIENT: Hamilton Events / DESIGNER: Jeff Fisher / ART DIRECTOR: Jeff Fisher

1466

LET'S TALK Coffee

1467

LIGER TELEVISION
King of The Content Jungle

1468

OHANA
CUP

1469

HISTORICAL SOCIETY OF THE
UNITED STATES DISTRICT COURT

WESTERN DISTRICT OF
OKLAHOMA

1470

1471

adventure

1472

1473

1466: CLIENT: Flatwater Fitness / DESIGNER: Chris Parks / ART DIRECTOR: Chris Parks
1467: COMPANY: Weather Control / CLIENT: Sustainable Harvest / DESIGNER: Josh Oakley
1468: COMPANY: ACTUART LP / CLIENT: Terri Mardi Ltd. / DESIGNER: Peter Vasvari / ART DIRECTOR: Peter Vasvari
1469: COMPANY: Star Group / CLIENT: AMNRL / DESIGNER: Scott Oeschger / ART DIRECTOR: Scott Oeschger
1470: COMPANY: ACTUART LP / CLIENT: Quantus / DESIGNER: Peter Vasvari / ART DIRECTOR: Peter Vasvari
1471: COMPANY: Chris Rooney Illustration/Design / CLIENT: Type A / DESIGNER: Chris Rooney
1472: COMPANY: ACTUART LP. / CLIENT: ESF, INC / DESIGNER: Peter Vasvari / ART DIRECTOR: Peter Vasvari
1473: COMPANY: Sussner Design Company / CLIENT: Sussner Design Company / DESIGNER: Ben Alpert / ART DIRECTOR: Derek Sussner

*a*        *b*

# Style Is Substance
## TRACY SABIN

Logos are the poetry of graphic design. They aim to say a lot with a minimum of means. This doesn't imply, however, that all logos should hew to one minimalist, modern design aesthetic. As early as the '50s, design firms like Push Pin Studios rebelled against the minimalism inspired by the Bauhaus, De Stijl, and the Swiss Style movements. For every minimalist masterpiece from the likes of Paul Rand or Saul Bass there were many works from lesser designers whose creations followed the dictates of minimalism but whose designs were, well, boring. Boring is not a desirable attribute for logos. Milton Glaser, Seymour Chwast, and the Push Pin Group demonstrated that a less than "pure" approach to design, drawing on stylistic trends from the past, from different regions of the world and from "high" or "low" cultural sources, could add a vital spark of interest and add to the content of the message as well.

Minimalism may be best suited to the logo designs of major corporations. But, let's face it, the vast majority of logo assignments are for small logos, for mom-and-pop concerns, one-time events, limited-duration housing developments, specialty products, charity organizations, and the like. For these modest entities and events, a different set of rules apply.

In other words, style can be one of the tools designers use to communicate in a shorthand way. Style is an aspect of the poetic minimalism of a logo. What lines of reasoning lead designers to choose one stylistic approach over another? The decision should not be arbitrary. Message, usage, and context are key factors.

Following are some examples from my experience.

I was hired by Conover Design to develop a logo for the SAM Awards, an architectural awards ceremony in San Diego that sponsors a themed festivity each year. The theme for 1990 was *C'est Magnifique* because it was the centenary of the start of the Belle Époque in Paris. The art director, David Conover, gave

*c*

*d*

*e*

*f*

instructions to create a logo in the style of an 1890s Parisian poster. That was the message of the logo. It was a fairly straight-forward process of researching the posters of the period, particularly the work of Toulouse-Lautrec and Jules Chéret, and coming up with a design inspired by those antecedents that would function well in the anticipated usages (fig. a). Those usages included a promotional poster, letterhead, programs, and other ancillary items. Because this was a one-time event and the reproduction methods for the various items were of a high quality, we could consider the option of a complex image. The communication of a fun event was of greater concern for this logo than the need to draw attention. That was the contextual aspect of the logo. The use of a historical style followed in an obvious way from the event itself.

The logos for Deleo tile used style to communicate in a more subtle way. Deleo creates a variety of specialty ceramic roof tiles. The art director, José Serrano from Mires Design established a plan, in consultation with other members of the creative team and the client, to fashion a logo for each of the tile varieties. José felt that the employment of a woodcut look would communicate a couple of key aspects of the product—that the tiles were based on regional historical patterns and that they were made with a high level of craftsmanship. That was the message. The primary use of these logos was to communicate Deleo's tradition-inspired, artisanal manufacturing process. The context resided both in drawing attention to the product in magazine advertising and in signaling the quality of the product on packaging and sample boxes (fig. b, c, d).

For some logos, drawing attention within a given context is the most important issue. Housing developments are mainly marketed through newspaper advertisements. The housing section of a newspaper is a competitive arena in which the reader's eyes scan pages quickly. Creating a minimalist logo for that environment may not be the best strategy. That's why the logo for the Amore housing development was conceived

by Greenhaus creative director, Craig Fuller and designers Jerry Sisti and Michael Grace, as something very different from the typical solution (fig. e). In the competition for quick scanning eyes, something that looks like a painting on stucco, rather than a simplistic logo, more effectively causes the reader to stop and pay attention. Usage and context are directly linked in this case. Secondarily, the stucco style and the depiction of an Italian villa points to the message that the houses in the development were inspired by Tuscan architecture.

Then, there are cases where a minimal approach is best. Odyssey, an imprint of Harcourt Inc., specialized in the publication of Children's Classics. Art Director Lisa Peters, helped formulate the strategy for the Odyssey branding. The message of the logo, embodied by the depiction of Odysseus' boat, is that reading the classics is an adventure. Because the logo was displayed on the spine of paperbacks it had to be very simple (fig. f). By treating all their cover designs in the same way, with the logo reversed out of black at the top of a solid white spine, Odyssey's books, such as the Mary Poppins series, called attention to themselves even when the books were displayed spine-out on a bookshelf. Here, the anticipated usage pushed the style toward simplicity. Like the Amore logo, usage and context were linked, but the choice of stylistic treatment was very different. The simple, bold, and daring solutions of the Bauhaus movement are one of the many stylistic trends a designer can pick and choose from to fulfill the aims of a particular design problem.

So, style can be more than just an arbitrary prettification. Style can communicate information and it can enhance the effectiveness of a logo within its anticipated context. It doesn't have to be a choice between style or substance. You can have both.

**NONSTOP**

1474

# THE GALAXY TriO

1475

1476

1477

FINE ART PORTRAITURE

*Kimberly Wylie*

1478

1479

O'Bannon Law

1480

HOLLY
BENDER
&
INTERIORS

1481

SUMMIT
CLIMBING

1482

MARTIN LUTHER
ACADEMY

1483

VIÑA
ESCONDIDA

*a*
*Silverwood*
*Community*

1484

TASTING BAR

1485

1486

EnglishPub

1487

1481: COMPANY: Chris Rooney Illustration/Design / CLIENT: Holly Bender / DESIGNER: Chris Rooney
1482: COMPANY: DesignUnion / CLIENT: Summit Climbing / DESIGNER: Renee Melton
1483: COMPANY: Schwartzrock Graphic Arts / CLIENT: 3.2.1, Inc. / DESIGNER: Sherwin Schwartzrock
1484: COMPANY: Tactix Creative, Inc. / CLIENT: Vina Escondida Estates / DESIGNER: Paul Howalt
1485: COMPANY: Banowetz & Company / CLIENT: Grain / Restaurant / Bar / DESIGNER: Sarah Terrell / ART DIRECTOR: Eric Venegas
1486: COMPANY: Adam Anderson / DESIGNER: Adam Anderson
1487: COMPANY: Enhive Creative Studio Pvt. Ltd. / CLIENT: Jarrod Swanger / DESIGNER: Debashis Nayak / ART DIRECTOR: Debashis Nayak

1488

1489

1490

1491

1492

**Greek Green Building Council**

1493

1494

1495

1496

1497

1498

**BRANDTHESPEAKER**

1499

1500

1501

1502

**MORE COPS.
MORE STOPS.**

1503

**1496:** COMPANY: Bailey Lauerman / CLIENT: Bailey Lauerman / DESIGNER: Brandon Oltman / ART DIRECTOR: Carter Weitz
**1497:** COMPANY: Bailey Lauerman / CLIENT: Bailey Lauerman / DESIGNER: Brandon Oltman / ART DIRECTOR: Carter Weitz
**1498:** COMPANY: Miles Design / CLIENT: HWC Engineering / DESIGNER: Brian K. Gray
**1499:** COMPANY: Dreambox Creative / CLIENT: Brand the Speaker / DESIGNER: Hans Bennewitz / ART DIRECTOR: Doru Bere
**1500:** COMPANY: Gardner Design / CLIENT: KETCH / DESIGNER: Brian Weins / ART DIRECTOR: Brian Miller
**1501:** COMPANY: Gyula Németh / CLIENT: / DESIGNER: Gyula Németh
**1502:** COMPANY: Bailey Lauerman / CLIENT: Bailey Lauerman / DESIGNER: Brandon Oltman / ART DIRECTOR: Carter Weitz
**1503:** COMPANY: Fernandez Studio / CLIENT: NHTSA / DESIGNER: Carlos Fernandez / ART DIRECTOR: Brian Potter

1504

1505

1506

1507

1508

1509

1510

**1504:** COMPANY: Logo Planet Laboratory / CLIENT: OliveIT / DESIGNER: Jeffrey Mardis
**1505:** COMPANY: Joseph Blalock Design Office / CLIENT: State of Texas / DESIGNER: Joseph Blalock
**1506:** COMPANY: Schwartzrock Graphic Arts / CLIENT: Group Publishing / DESIGNER: Sherwin Schwartzrock
**1507:** COMPANY: Jay Vigon Design / CLIENT: Lightstorm Entertainment / DESIGNER: Jay Vigon / ART DIRECTOR: Jay Vigon
**1508:** COMPANY: Fernandez Studio / CLIENT: The Palladium / DESIGNER: Carlos Fernandez / ART DIRECTOR: Mike Wilson
**1509:** COMPANY: Mirko Ilić Corp. / CLIENT: Jewish Film Festival / DESIGNER: Mirko Ilić / ART DIRECTOR: Mirko Ilić
**1510:** COMPANY: Michael Doret Graphic Design / CLIENT: Howard Marks Adv. / DESIGNER: Michael Doret / ART DIRECTOR: Dennis Woloch

CHRYSLER *financial*™

1511

1512

1513

1514

1515

1516

**1511:** COMPANY: Gardner Design / CLIENT: Chrysler Financial / DESIGNER: Ty Wilkins / ART DIRECTOR: Brian Miller
**1512:** COMPANY: Baji Group / CLIENT: Phoenix Design Week / DESIGNER: Jonny Ashcroft
**1513:** COMPANY: leightonhubbell.com / CLIENT: Oney Rooding / DESIGNER: Leighton Hubbell / ART DIRECTOR: Leighton Hubbell
**1514:** COMPANY: Mirko Ilić Corp. / CLIENT: Atlas Print Solutions / DESIGNER: Mirko Ilić / ART DIRECTOR: Mirko Ilić
**1515:** COMPANY: Fernandez Studio / CLIENT: Moore IT Services / DESIGNER: Carlos Fernandez / ART DIRECTOR: Carlos Fernandez
**1516:** COMPANY: Flight Deck Creative / CLIENT: Network Neighborhood / DESIGNER: Jason Rahn / ART DIRECTOR: Jason Rahn

1517

**BRANCH**
ENTERPRISES

1518

1519

**BRAVIANT**

1520

1521

**kafer**
musical instruments

1522

The Joseph School

1523

**NORTH**
CONSTRUCTION

1524

**1517:** CLIENT: New Works Design Group / DESIGNER: Muamer ADILOVIC / ART DIRECTOR: Muamer ADILOVIC
**1518:** COMPANY: Timber Design Co. / DESIGNER: Lars Lawson
**1519:** COMPANY: Gravitate Design Studio / DESIGNER: Marc Neidlinger / ART DIRECTOR: Marc Neidlinger
**1520:** COMPANY: Sean Heisler / CLIENT: Braviant / DESIGNER: Sean Heisler / ART DIRECTOR: Sean Heisler
**1521:** COMPANY: Pollard Design / DESIGNER: Jeff Pollard
**1522:** CLIENT: Kafer / DESIGNER: Artem Dvorzhak
**1523:** COMPANY: Lewis Communications / CLIENT: The Joseph School / DESIGNER: Robert Froedge / ART DIRECTOR: Robert Froedge
**1524:** COMPANY: Sean Heisler / CLIENT: North Construction / DESIGNER: Sean Heisler / ART DIRECTOR: Sean Heisler

**POTENTIALYZE**
Tap your potential. Top your results.

1525

1526

1527

1528

1529

1530

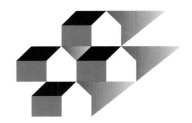

1531

mystic

1532

**1525:** COMPANY: Jeremy Slagle Graphic Desogn / CLIENT: Potentialyze / DESIGNER: Jeremy Slagle / ART DIRECTOR: Jeremy Slagle
**1526:** COMPANY: R&R Partners / CLIENT: personal / DESIGNER: Randy Heil / ART DIRECTOR: Randy Heil
**1527:** COMPANY: Schwartzrock Graphic Arts / CLIENT: Schwartzrock Graphic Arts / DESIGNER: Sherwin Schwartzrock
**1528:** COMPANY: Chris Rooney Illustration/Design / CLIENT: San Francisco Bay Area Water Transit / DESIGNER: Chris Rooney / ART DIRECTOR: Jef Loyola, The M-Line
**1529:** COMPANY: Mint / CLIENT: Luum / DESIGNER: Bryan Danknich / ART DIRECTOR: Mike Calkins
**1530:** COMPANY: Schwartzrock Graphic Arts / CLIENT: Delphax / DESIGNER: Sherwin Schwartzrock
**1531:** COMPANY: Pollard Design / DESIGNER: Jeff Pollard
**1532:** COMPANY: Mattson Creative / DESIGNER: Ty Mattson

1533

1534

1535

1536

1537

1538

1539

**1533:** COMPANY: Fairchild Creative / CLIENT: Fairchild Creative / DESIGNER: Douglas Fairchild / ART DIRECTOR: Douglas Fairchild
**1534:** CLIENT: Strong House Residencies / DESIGNER: Kyle Dingman
**1535:** COMPANY: Star Group / CLIENT: Star Group / DESIGNER: Scott Oeschger / ART DIRECTOR: Scott Oeschger
**1536:** COMPANY: Owen Jones Design / CLIENT: Personal Project / DESIGNER: Owen Jones / ART DIRECTOR: Owen Jones
**1537:** COMPANY: BrandLtd.com / CLIENT: Brand Athletic Team for Spartan Race / DESIGNER: Jordan Kabalka / ART DIRECTOR: Virginia Martino
**1538:** CLIENT: Global Air Force Museum / DESIGNER: Jake Dugard
**1539:** COMPANY: Joseph Blalock Design Office / CLIENT: Raven Styling / DESIGNER: Joseph Blalock

1540

1541

1542

1543

1544

1545

1546

1540: COMPANY: Schwartzrock Graphic Arts / CLIENT: MN Health and Housing Association / DESIGNER: Sherwin Schwartzrock
1541: COMPANY: Invisible Creature / CLIENT: All American Rejects / DESIGNER: Ryan Clark / ART DIRECTOR: Ryan Clark
1542: COMPANY: Richard Hejsak / CLIENT: Service Works Global / DESIGNER: Richard Hejsak
1543: COMPANY: Tactix Creative, Inc. / CLIENT: Haven Homes / DESIGNER: Cam Stewart
1544: COMPANY: Pollard Design / DESIGNER: Jeff Pollard
1545: COMPANY: Funnel Design Group / CLIENT: Chevy Band Van / DESIGNER: Taylor Good
1546: COMPANY: chameleon design / CLIENT: Petra Krajcsovicsova / DESIGNER: Tomas Vateha / ART DIRECTOR: Tomas Vateha

# Index

**Greteman Group, USA**
*www.gretemangroup.com*
590, 829, 889, 946, 950, 953,
965, 980, 984, 986, 1020, 1024,
1026, 1031, 1136, 1248, 1249,
1315, 1316, 1378

**Grupo Habermas Comunicacion, Spain**
*www.grupohabermas.com*
110

**Gyula Németh, Hungary**
*www.gynemeth.com*
708, 792, 888, 892, 951, 958,
970, 1030, 1078, 1081, 1086,
1087, 1091, 1144, 1194, 1196,
1198, 1200, 1201, 1317, 1318,
1379, 1381, 1430, 1440, 1501

**H2 Design of Texas, USA**
*http://www.hoyth.com*
1010, 1168, 1230, 1292

**Hatch Design, USA**
*www.hatchsf.com*
155, 160, 392, 393, 771, 832,
1139, 1141, 1325, 1380, 1382

**Hayes Image, Australia**
*www.hayesimage.com.au*
759, 760, 780, 812, 813, 834

**Holy Cow Creative, USA**
*www.holycow.org*
1384, 1412

**idgroup, USA**
*www.idgrouprsa.com*
763, 770

**Invisible Creature, USA**
*www.invisiblecreature.com*
80, 88, 95, 139, 309, 318, 335,
376, 432, 492, 501, 540, 611,
736, 738, 805, 861, 917, 998,
1109, 1111, 1159, 1170, 1352,
1424, 1458, 1541

**J. Sayles Design Co., USA**
*www.saylesdesign.com*
170, 415, 443, 534, 609, 612,
666, 714, 734, 769, 779, 793,
787, 807, 840, 901, 913, 968,
969, 971, 1006, 1033, 1042,
1083, 1089, 1138, 1210, 1212,
1213, 1221, 1234, 1260, 1322,
1398

**Jajo, USA**
*www.jajo.net*
676

**Jake Dugard, USA**
*www.jakedugard.com*
1538

**Jake Thompson, UK**
*www.behance.net/ja-kethompson*
1385

**Janus, Serbia**
*www.jmg.rs*
1355

**Jared Granger, USA**
*www.jaredgranger.com*
112, 830, 838, 857, 863, 1164,
1308

**Jay Vigon Design, USA**
*www.jayvigon.com*
1037, 1383, 1507

**Jeff Andrews Design, USA**
*www.jeffandrewsdesign.com*
867

**Jeff Fisher LogoMotives, USA**
*www.jfisherlogomotives.com*
1465

**Jeremy Slagle Graphic Design, USA**
*www.jeremyslagle.com*
247, 254, 438, 548, 709, 992,
1034, 1047, 1094, 1099, 1155,
1182, 1275, 1279, 1525

**Jon Flaming Design, USA**
*www.jonflaming.com*
29, 64, 122, 148, 178, 242, 417,
421, 422, 424–426, 472, 475,
478, 484, 535, 536, 537, 542,
593, 598, 603, 654, 661, 711,
719, 773, 791, 831, 839, 896,
899, 1040, 1090, 1206

**Joseph Blalock Design Office, USA**
*www.josephblalock.com*
156, 165, 172, 176, 872, 877,
884, 1145, 1205, 1208, 1209,
1214, 1215, 1255–1259, 1319,
1320, 1437, 1505, 1539

**Jude Landry, USA**
*www.judelandry.com*
1045, 1276, 1391

**Julian Hrankov, Germany**
*www.julianhrankov.com*
876, 1357

**Kim Chan, USA**
*www.kimchan.net*
1441

**Knoed Creative, USA**
*www.knoed.com*
4, 608, 731

**Krauss + Henkhaus + Krause GbR, Germany**
*www.falconwhite.com*
836

**Kris Bazen Creative, USA**
*www.krisbazen.com*
479, 848, 849, 905, 1036, 1262

**Kyle Dingman, USA**
*www.kyledingman.com*
1012, 1534

**Kyle Richardson, USA**
*www.enrichdesign.us*
1171

**Lanky Design, Italy**
*www.lankydesign.com*
1263

**leightonhubbell.com, USA**
*http://www.leightonhubbell.com*
189, 201, 214, 394, 624, 627,
651, 653, 730, 796, 844, 847,
903, 904, 906, 909, 959, 960,
962, 967, 973, 1038, 1046,
1048, 1082, 1098, 1143, 1147,
1218–1220, 1149, 1150, 1211,
1217, 1222, 1224, 1240, 1264,
1330, 1386–1389, 1390,
1392–1394, 1396, 1442, 1444,
1513

**Lethcoe Design, USA**
671

**Lewis Communications, USA**
*www.lewiscommunications.com*
605, 607, 1338, 1523

**Little, USA**
*www.littleonline.com*
400

**Logo Planet Laboratory, USA**
*http://www.logoplanetlab.com*
55, 717, 768, 1137, 1207, 1246,
1324, 1504

**Logopond, Ukraine**
*http://logopond.com/artdemix*
554, 615, 737, 809, 1096, 1447,
1450, 1522

**Logo Turn, USA**
*www.logoturn.com/gregory-grigoriou*
469

**Luke Bott Design & Illustration, USA**
*www.lukebott.com*
21, 33, 60, 132, 244, 427, 480,
1236

**M3 Advertising Design, USA**
*www.m3ad.com*
482, 1339

**Matt Lehman Studio, USA**
*www.mattlehmanstudio.com*
262, 403, 407, 673, 701, 1395

**Mattson Creative, USA**
*www.mattsoncreative.com*
185, 188, 507, 915, 1058, 1158,
1344, 1454, 1532

**Melodic Virtue, USA**
*www.melodicvirtue.com*
5, 17, 19, 183

**Michael Doret Graphic Design, USA**
*http://www.michaeldoret.com*
430, 604, 613, 797, 908, 987,
991, 1095, 1267, 1510

**Michael Spitz Design, USA**
*www.michaelspitz.com*
358

**Mike Jones, USA**
*www.dribble.com/bucket826*
92, 171, 230, 235,

**Miles Design, USA**
*www.milesdesign.com*
837, 858, 1304, 1498

# Index

**The Joe Bosack Graphic Design Co., USA**
*www.joebosack.com*
473, 477, 539, 602, 655, 659, 662, 667, 705, 716, 718, 720, 746, 781, 784, 786, 789, 794, 826, 895, 961, 964, 997, 1039, 1043, 1080, 1135, 1142, 1148, 1203, 1204, 1252, 1253, 1254, 1323

**The Mahoney Studio, USA**
*www.themahoney.com*
1328, 1402

**Thinkcreative Design, Australia**
*www.thinkcreative.net.au/#/home*
134

**Thrillustrate, USA**
*www.shanecawthon.carbon-made.com*
503, 547, 665, 995, 1054, 1055, 1336

**Throttle Design Mechanics, USA**
*www.ThrottleDM.com*
356, 366, 549, 814, 860, 1056, 1105, 1281

**Tim Frame Design, USA**
*www.timframe.com*
75, 77, 553, 133, 182, 187, 191, 243, 248, 308, 322, 361, 368, 428, 436, 550, 592

**Timber Design Co., USA**
*www.timberdesignco.com*
504, 616, 674, 675, 808, 910, 1057, 1285, 1400, 1518

**Tortoiseshell Black, UK**
*www.tsbcreative.co.uk*
756

**Touchwood Design Inc., Canada**
*www.touchwooddesign.com*
866, 882

**Trainor Design, USA**
*www.trainor-design.com*
111, 460

**TY Design, USA**
*www.tywilkins.com*
203, 319, 511, 697, 703, 801, 1327, 1457

**U! Creative, Inc., USA**
*www.ucreate.us*
32, 67, 85, 94, 98, 143, 200, 245, 362–365, 846, 855

**Varsity Mascot Company, USA**
*www.varsitymascot.com*
557, 560, 678, 722, 862, 881, 1227, 1229, 1283

**Voov Ltd., Hungary**
*www.voov.hu*
413, 875, 932, 1008, 1235

**Weather Control, USA**
*www.weatherctrl.com*
249, 371, 509, 520, 606, 725, 739, 856, 1059, 1061, 1225, 1282, 1286, 1288, 1467, 1408

**WORKtoDATE (www.worktodate.com), USA**
*www.worktodate.com*
124, 135, 365, `025, 1376, 1432

**Yona Lee Design Studio, Switzerland**
*www.yonalee.com*
34, 36

# About the Authors

Paul Howalt is creative director and partner at Tactix Creative in Mesa, Arizona, a branding firm specializing in identity development.

Over the last twenty-three years, he has had the privilege of working with many of the world's most beloved and influential brands. Clients include Mtv, Levi's, Disney, HBO, Target, Hasbro, Pepsi, and IBM.

Paul has juried design competitions, spoken at industry-related events and written for numerous design publications. His work has been awarded multiple awards in every major national design competition.

He is also an accomplished illustrator and photographer.

www.tactixcreative.com

Von Glitschka is principal of Glitschka Studios, a multidisciplinary creative firm. The studio shines as a hired creative resource for numerous ad agencies, design firms, and in-house corporate art departments internationally.

Von is an illustrative designer whose work reflects a symbiotic relationship between design and illustration in order to create a diverse range of projects for some of the worlds most respected companies and brands.

Glitschka Studios exuberant graphics have garnered numerous design and illustration awards. Von is a popular speaker on the topic of design and creativity, brand identity, marketing, and is an adjunct professor of digital illustration and author of five books.

www.vonglitschka.com